Mr Grinza

A fellow birder and
Audubon member

Best wishes.

Mike Foster

The Ties That Bind

Birds, Nature and Us

MIKE F. FOSTER

authorHOUSE®

AuthorHouse™
1663 Liberty Drive
Bloomington, IN 47403
www.authorhouse.com
Phone: 1-800-839-8640

First published by AuthorHouse 10/4/2010

ISBN: 978-1-4520-7617-1 (hc)
ISBN: 978-1-4520-7618-8 (sc)
ISBN: 978-1-4520-7619-5 (e)

Library of Congress Control Number: 2010913186

Printed in the United States of America

This book is printed on acid-free paper.

THE AUTHOR WISHES TO ACKNOWLEDGE the following publications in which earlier versions of some of these essays first appeared. "A Tale of Two Planets" was part of *Colorado Environmental Report* (Spring 2005), the quarterly newsletter of the Colorado Environmental Coalition. "Plumbing and Virtue" was published in the December 2007 issue of *The Dipper*, the newsletter of The Evergreen Naturalists Audubon Society, as was "Let There Be CFLs," in the January/February 2008 issue. "Open Space and Natural History" had its debut in the March 2008 issue of *The Lark Bunting*, the newsletter of Denver Field Ornithologists. The following also came out in *The Lark Bunting*, in monthly succession between May and November 2008: "Global Warming, Part One," "Global Warming, Part Two," "Two Worlds of Birding," "How Much is Enough?" "The Beauty *Is* the Beast," "Attitudes 101," and "Attitudes 301." "Leaves Are Us" appeared as "The Philosopher" in *Trail and Timberline* (Winter 2009-2010), the magazine of the Colorado Mountain Club.

This book is for:

Sheila Ray Duranso

Alice Levine, and

Brwyn Harris Downing

Table of Contents

I. Introduction

ONE DAY AT THE AGE of ten or so, a boy found himself in the top branches of an apple tree, which grew in the back yard of his grandparents' home. He often took pleasure in watching birds and fantasizing about being one. How would a worm taste? He tried one. He did not repeat the experiment, but that didn't stop him from admiring their skills as hunters, their superb aerobatics, and most of all their fierce confidence and graceful posture. Compared to these talented creatures, the boy felt inadequate. He was a disoriented, confused youth, the sort who set fire to vacant lots, or placed a running hose in the open basement window of a neighbor whose noisy, aggressive dog he disliked.

The boy found little comfort in the company of humans, but a soothing wholeness when surrounded by birds. He yearned to be a bird. He pursued them, conversed with them, and tried to imagine what each was thinking. He obscured himself in order to observe them unawares. The mother of a playmate described him to her daughters as "an Indian; he is so quiet and moves so deliberately. One moment you see him, the next moment he has disappeared somewhere in the yard"—a flattering portrait the boy cherished and tried to embody.

Which was how he came to be in the upper branches of that apple tree. A number of robins had shown a preference for some bug there, and he wanted to know more. Naturally, as soon as he climbed into the tree, the robins went elsewhere, which proved a disappointment. Despite his fascination for them, it had not occurred to him that birds might have

1

intentions that conflicted with his own. He was sad that they chose to scorn his curiosity, but they seemed to be trying to tell him something: "We are different from you. We are not your friends, even if you like us. But if you don't interfere, we may tolerate you, allow you to look, follow us around, and do the other silly things you do." It was a useful lesson, but an incomplete one. It taught of differences and separation, but it ignored the wider unity of all living things.

And now, many years later, birds are still giving lessons, not just to bird nuts like me, but to any humans sensitive enough to be appalled at the sight of pelicans covered with slimy, feather-destroying, life-snuffing oil that exploded from the floor of the Gulf of Mexico in the spring of 2010. Similar sights appalled us back in 1989, when the oil tanker Exxon Valdez went aground and despoiled Prince William Sound and the North Gulf of Alaska. Despite the "clean-up," large quantities of toxic oil remain in the soils and beaches, on the rocks and shrubs and plants, and in the bodies of countless species along the southern coast of Alaska. Such oil disasters are not rare events if you consider the long history of oil exploitation, but these two happened in our own back yard. We tend to ignore the impact of such disasters in the back yards of other people or other species.

Oil is not the only problem. Every time we create a suburb or a strip mall or an industrial park, we destroy the homes and livelihoods of birds and animals who used to live there, creatures who are the true pioneers. Every time we build skyscrapers or cell phone towers or wind turbines, we are creating death traps for birds. The poisons we pour on our weeds annihilate birds and other creatures. The cats we love and spoil become bird killers if allowed to prowl outdoors. Our native plants and shrubs and trees are the natural homes and breeding grounds for numerous birds, places where they find most of their food, but some of our favorite garden plants are exotics that crowd out the native flora.

Birds are more than just canaries in the coal mine. As indicator species they are identifying all the habitats and communities and ecosystems that are in trouble today. Of course, the larger message is that if natural areas and systems are in trouble, humans are in trouble, too, because we are part of the natural world. I speak on behalf of birds and Nature, to emphasize our mutual links and needs, and to make the simple point that loving birds is in our own best interests.

It is easy to love birds. Just notice them. Gorgeous in their varied plumages, they delight the eye. Their songs gladden and sadden, roar and reverberate, enchant and excite. Their swooping and soaring amazes, filling us with awe and not a little envy. They accomplish feats with a beak for which we require two arms, two hands, and ten fingers. Traditionally, they have prospered in most habitats on Earth, yet many disdain a single residence. They travel with the seasons, some visiting only in the next county or state, while others migrate tens of thousands of miles every year. Some use tools, others can count, many can identify individual humans, just as we love to ID them. The more you notice birds—the diversity of their nests or mating habits or food resources—the more fascinating their versatile lifestyles become.

To save birds and to preserve the planet we must first heal ourselves, because as intolerance and selfishness demonstrate every day, humanity is in trouble with itself. We can begin to save ourselves by realizing that our fate is inextricably linked to that of the natural world. We can begin to heal our natural environment by relearning cooperation, mutual respect, and generosity of spirit—virtues which will reinforce our intimate and infinite ties to Mother Nature. Rescuing Nature while redeeming ourselves is largely a matter of changing attitudes.

Unfortunately, the pace and focus of modern life work against an awareness of the natural world, and our attitudes toward it. In our predominantly urban culture, we are stimulated by a nonstop media, we are flooded with information from the Internet, but increasingly we connect to Nature and to each other through our isolated computer stations, iPods, cell phones, Facebook, or Twitter. We are overlooking the life-altering rewards that accompany openhearted encounters with Nature.

But if you are willing to give Mother Nature a chance, you will find her a brilliant teacher and the most powerful advocate. She recruited me to her cause through direct encounters, a recounting of which I hope will encourage you to do your own noticing, so that you, too, will enlist in the cause of saving birds and Nature and ourselves.

A contemporary of Shakespeare once called him an "upstart crow."

I like to think of myself in that way. I'm no Shakespeare, but I am an upstart, and I'll gladly accept the association with brother crow. I am a nature advocate confident enough to think he might change some attitudes and habits. I am a native son bold enough to question the received wisdom regarding growth and the consumer economy. I am compelled to write because I feel I have put my finger on what millions of others are feeling but not yet expressing. By training I am a professional historian, by inclination a dedicated amateur naturalist. Much of what I have to say you will not find in other books on Nature, the environment, or birds. The questions I raise in these essays probe subjects most of us prefer to ignore, for example: Why are so many Americans still denying their role in global warming? How is the "energy crisis" mostly a matter of attitudes? What would bacteria like to tell us? Why is water shortage a moral issue?

Cartoon character Pogo (author Walt Kelly) once said: "We have met the enemy, and he is us." The American public is intoxicated—hallucinating that it can prosper while gorging on consumer goods and leisure-time amusements. If we want to save birds and Nature, and rehabilitate ourselves, we must stop chasing mirages of super abundance and excessive wealth.

I have written these essays for Pogo's "us," among whom I include myself. We are the millions of Americans who pay lip service to protecting Nature, but fail to walk the talk. We are the fortunate branch of the middle class, who often take for granted our education, our security, and our prosperity, without stopping to consider that the consumer society that has brought us so much comfort and leisure is also undermining the natural world, the ultimate source of our good fortune. Our thoughtless behaviors stem from myopia, but attitudes can change if confronted with a wake-up call.

Naturally, people don't like to hear that they are despoiling the planet. Telling them so may not impel them to change. I accept that *some* people will not change, no matter how serious the circumstances, just as some people when told they have lung cancer or emphysema will go on smoking. But more pragmatic people are rolling up their sleeves and getting involved because they understand the stakes.

Of course, there are selfish, greedy, even evil people in the world, but I believe that our indifference toward Mother Nature derives more from laziness, ignorance, or force of habit than from more sinister motives. Short-sighted folk have always opposed the common good. But idealists and reformers and genuine statesmen display our better selves. The struggle to protect Nature while preserving human prosperity will not be won by a clash of Saints vs. Ogres. It will be won, if at all, by the steady, unspectacular efforts of ordinary citizens who use their growing awareness and caring to overthrow convenient myths and long-held prejudices. The beauty and practicality of an environmental perspective is that it demonstrates connectivity, enables tolerance, and promotes cooperation.

2. Early Birds

CARDINALS FLOURISH IN THE AMERICAN Midwest—the birds, that is. The other kind parade around Vatican City, but they are not my concern here. A few populations of *Cardinalis cardinalis* live near the eastern edge of Colorado, where they inhabit shrubs and thickets, preferably near a stream, and they eat seeds, fruit, and insects. But a cardinal near the Front Range of Colorado, where most of the population of the state resides, and where I make my home in a suburb of Denver, is a rare bird indeed.

Rare or not, there he was, taking seeds from a feeder. Not just any feeder, but one in the back yard of my friends Marge and Sam Romberger. Their yard abuts a trail along the northeastern flank of South Table Mountain, a path that I walk regularly in all seasons. This was the winter of 2003-04, an even more unusual time for a male cardinal to appear in the Denver area. I had not seen the bird during previous walks that winter, and I might have missed him had Marge not phoned me with news of her exotic visitor.

I like to think I would have found the cardinal anyway, sooner or later, because he stayed all winter, from roughly November through March. Was it mere coincidence that he chose a location along a trail I walked regularly? And was it just coincidence that he stayed all winter, instead of reorienting his internal compass and scooting back to Lamar, or some suitable place along Colorado's eastern border? Of course, it was entirely coincidence, but I like to stay open to the seductions of imagination. I flattered myself that this cardinal made his surprising appearance to find me, and to allow me to reconnect with him.

After all, cardinals and I go back a long way together. Specifically, we go back to my early boyhood, to around the age of nine, and to the jovial Irishman who was my grandfather. This grandfather exerted the most powerful influence on my early years, and, for better or worse, his legacies have profoundly shaped the course of my life. Because he was an avid baseball fan, the family had box seats for the Denver Bears, at first a Class A team, later a Triple A feeder of the New York Yankees. Red was my favorite color at the time, and when I discovered a baseball team called the St. Louis Cardinals, instantly I became a fan of the Redbirds. I've favored them ever since. So, naturally, when Granddad and I formed the habit of tossing a baseball every morning while I waited for the school bus, I wore a Cardinals' cap. I still have one. Shortly after falling under the spell of the Cardinals, my grandmother (the wife of the Irishman) gave me a realistic sculpture of the male cardinal, carved in wood, perfectly colored, and posed on a branch. Somehow I lost the original, but I replaced it with a reasonable facsimile that still reposes in my study.

In short order I assimilated some of Granddad's other interests. He had season tickets for the Denver Symphony and often invited me to accompany him on Thursday evenings. He had tickets to Mammoth Gardens, where professional wrestlers mauled each other. I was so taken with one gladiator that when he lost I stood up and shouted, "Don't worry, you'll get him next time." Having acted on impulse, I suddenly felt totally embarrassed, especially as the fans surrounding us grew oddly quiet. The gladiator looked astonished, but smiled and waved, to the amusement of the crowd. On an automobile trip to California (this was long before interstate highways), I sat in Granddad's lap and steered while he manipulated the pedals. Every night we ate well-done steak and apple pie à la mode. Thanks to him I cast my first dry fly into the clear, icy waters of a stream that feeds the mighty Colorado River. With him I observed my first professional theatrical production. And as his inconspicuous understudy, I watched in fascination as he flirted outrageously with beautiful women. No doubt prompted by his amorous example, I decided I needed a beautiful woman of my own, and at least I had the boldness to aim high. I fell for the young film actress Elizabeth Taylor, whose seductive romps in "National Velvet" inspired my first libidinous fantasies. Had there not been other birds in my life, I might never have become a serious stalker of the Class Aves.

But a month shy of my thirteenth birthday I boarded the Burlington Zephyr in Denver with a profound sense of betrayal. I was bound for a New England prep school, my grandfather, the chief proponent of this unwelcome relocation, accompanying me. Although we enjoyed an adventurous trip—watching Satchel Paige pitch against the Chicago White Sox, seeing my first Broadway theatre production, and scarfing down lots of steak and apple pie—the day he left me at school I felt utterly abandoned once again. The first time had been five years before, when my mother died of pneumonia, and I and a younger half brother and half sister went to live with her parents.

The earliest bird to capture my attention in person was a hummingbird, two in fact. They began building a nest on a branch not six feet from the upstairs bathroom window of my grandparents' home. Instantly upon meeting them, and without realizing it, I became a naturalist. Ever since that time birds have been tightening their grasp on my soul, sometimes allowing me a leisurely accumulation of knowledge, at other times forcefully demanding a spurt in my curiosity.

My grandmother was the first to notice the hummers. Nana was one of those non-liberated women, typical of her generation in preferring the role of homemaker (more like the Duchess of Denver in her case), but atypical in that she rose above her privileged childhood and her country-club marriage on the strength of her own merits and mustard.

At that age I was somewhat shorter than my diminutive grandmother, so I had to stand on the toilet, with the seat cover down, to see out the window and watch the hummingbirds. I had never experienced anything like them. One bird oozed a vibrant kaleidoscope of colors on the throat, which varied from red to purple to nearly black. Both birds wore coats of shimmering emerald on their backs, and flashed red and orange from uncertain parts of their bodies.

Both birds participated in constructing the nest, and when they flew away in search of more material I went ballistic, fearing they would never come back. Of course, they did, and eventually I could sense a purpose in their brief landings. We watched them weave bits of grass, spider webs, and other silky, slender materials into a perfectly cupped nest, neatly anchored in the crotch of two small branches. Then came the endless period of incubation. Time after time when I looked out the window, the female, partially hidden, rested quietly, beak raised but scarcely moving. The male buzzed in for brief moments, and seemed to be dueling with his mate. Nana explained that he was providing her with food, probably nectar, since she could not move until her babies hatched.

Nana purchased a bird guide, which she often read aloud while I kept watch out the window. The book told us absolutely nothing about what was going on at the nest. It did, however, help us distinguish the male from the female. On the strength of comparisons between what we saw and what the book showed, we tagged our birds as ruby-throated hummingbirds. Neither of us realized that the glittering colors of hummingbirds varied considerably according to the intensity and angle of light, or that several hummingbirds can look nearly the same, depending on the light. Our book lacked range maps, else we would likely have identified our tiny guests as broad-tailed hummingbirds. But a decisive identification was the least of our concerns.

Finally, two chicks emerged, which initiated a frenzied feeding cycle. Because their nest sat slightly above our line of sight, we never saw the chicks until they were already well into their growth. They appeared drab and colorless compared to their parents. From the time they first poked their heads above the side of the nest, the two nestlings already seemed large. And hungry. And impatient. The parents sortied away then back in rapid succession, taking turns foraging for nectar, insects, and various unidentified invertebrates to satisfy two voracious chicks. The chicks seemed to grow by the day.

While my grandfather and I had been bonding through adventurous discoveries, with my grandmother the bonding linked birds with family. She spoke a lot about the similarity of birds and humans. Given my lively imagination, I began to see those birds as much more than a model of family togetherness. They invited me to escape to a whole new universe, a mysterious but charming place that suggested entirely different lessons than the ones a troubled and troublesome youngster had been reluctantly absorbing.

One day, still dependent on their parents, the two fledglings launched themselves from nest to branch, and from branch to branch in something resembling flight for what seemed the better part of a morning. Then they suddenly disappeared, as did the parents. Did they survive? Where did they go? I never knew, but I never forgot them. I thought of them periodically, especially again about a year later, in that memorable day in the apple tree, when I had an epiphany: if I stuck with the birds, I would be all right. Like most epiphanies, it didn't provide a table of contents, but its meaning was unmistakable and its message reassuring. Especially in the unhappy years of boarding school soon to follow, I often thought of the hummingbirds and realized that, like them, I was now out of the nest and had to learn to cope on my own.

Oddly, my passion for birds and wildlife failed to influence my choice of a career. By the time I completed high school I had pulled myself together sufficiently to get into a good college, where I blossomed intellectually and took pleasure in the widest samplings of the curriculum. After two years as an instructor in a boys' preparatory school, I decided I wanted to be a historian. Accordingly, after a year of independent study in Europe, I enrolled at Columbia University and became a New Yorker. I enjoyed graduate school enormously, and I was looking forward to becoming a history professor. Or was I?

Just after passing my oral exams, and before committing to a dissertation topic, one of those little bubbles of doubt wiggled to the surface of my consciousness. Was the career of historian what I really wanted? Would the culture of academia be congenial? To help resolve such questions, I found a career-counseling firm in downtown New York and submitted to a week's intensive examination of myself, my skills, my background, and my goals. The counselor who went over the results with me had a lot to say, but mostly I remember his two summarizing remarks. "You asked us to assess your abilities, and consider how compatible you would be to the life of a scholar. Well, you seem to be bright enough, you obviously love research, and you already write pretty well, so we foresee no problems there." Naturally, I was delighted. Then taken aback, abruptly, as he continued, "What puzzles us is, how did you decide on becoming a historian? All your interests point in the direction of the natural sciences. Why aren't you a biologist?"

Why indeed? The answer seemed to be that despite a genuine love of natural history, I had no credentials or training in the field. I didn't know a *Bacillus* from a *Boletus*. Nor did I foresee the explosion of interest in ecology that would erupt across the nation not long after I became a fully fledged historian. So, three years later, like a lot of young scholars freshly minted with two advanced degrees, and by then having a wife and two children, I decided to get on with my career. Over the next decade that career took me to England, California, Illinois, then back to Colorado. At every stop along the way I bought bird guides and, on my own, got acquainted with the local avifauna. Once back in Colorado I joined several local Audubon societies, learned from more experienced naturalists, then eventually began leading birding trips myself.

While re-discovering my passion for Nature, and beginning to do something about it, I was finding satisfying work in the non-profit sector that was a liberating and socially engaging contrast to the often self-absorbed isolation of academia. Meanwhile, after twelve years of marriage, my first wife and I agreed to divorce. Over the next three decades I explored intimate relationships, one at a time, with a variety of compelling women. The box score reads as follows: two more marriages, two cohabitations (one brief, the other rather longer), several affairs, a few romances, and a number of companionable interludes, some of which blossomed into lasting friendships. After all that, what I finally realized in my sixties was what my daughter's generation seemed to know innately: that marriage is not for everyone, and there is no shame in defying convention when it means being true to yourself.

Returning to Colorado encouraged me to return to a pre-teen love of mountain climbing, and I began a systematic quest to climb challenging high peaks in the state, including all fifty-four of the fourteen-thousand footers. Mountains also, as they are wont to do, penetrated my soul through their mysteries. The mystery of rock, for instance: squeezing thousands of tiny, rough grains of mineral, black and white and gray, into solid fists; or piling up, one on top of another, smooth layer cakes of limestone, yellow and brown and dusty, then bending them into painful postures. The mystery of space: how, the closer you approach it, the more a summit recedes behind false summits you never saw from below, and how, once you stand on its crest, the summit itself disappears, leaving you adrift in an ocean of near and far peaks whose distances puzzle and whose dimensions baffle. The mystery of weather: wind herding clouds in and out of ravines, over and under ridges, until you question the position of immobile rock you saw just moments before, while rain turns scenic crags into slippery phantoms, and snow hides treacherous footing under a blanket of blinding white.

Roaming around the mountains stimulated my curiosity about the climbers, scientists, and artists who had preceded me there, so I began researching the lives of various American naturalists. I was particularly drawn to Ferdinand Vandeveer Hayden (1828-1887), a man who profoundly shaped the American West, and our conception of it, yet a mysterious man with a tarnished reputation. Sensing there was more to this strange genius than historians had discovered, I resolved to give my curiosity its sway. The result was the first full biography of his life. It was the peak experience of my life so far. The more I learned about Hayden and other naturalists, the more I realized I was one, and this prompted me (over forty years after earning a Bachelor's degree) to go back to school to get grounded in the natural sciences. I started taking biology courses at the University of Colorado: first the basics, then ecology, then evolution, finally ornithology.

These courses woke me up to some startling facts. I learned that biodiversity (short for biological diversity) is declining rapidly around the world, for numerous species. For birds this means that a third of the species now alive, or more, may disappear before the end of the present century. The traditional challenges facing birds and all life forms (competition, predation, and parasitism) amount to only a small fraction of the threats posed by humans, considering the countless ways we impact, directly and indirectly, all the planet's ecosystems. Too often, humans ignore the unique and irreplaceable gifts of Nature. Even when we are sensitive to the needs of creatures, our soaring population results in accelerated destruction and degradation of natural habitats.

Emboldened by such knowledge, I began writing popular essays on birds. Over the years since the cardinal and the hummingbirds, I had become enamored of a number of other birds: the blue jay, magpie, red-headed woodpecker, and marsh hawk (still a better name than northern harrier), to name only my favorites. I also carried out modest research projects on birds—their occurrence over different years at favorite sites, their comparative abundance at those and similar sites over longer periods of time, their habitat affiliations and unusual nesting locations.

My fraternizing with the rock wren began some forty years ago, during my active days as a mountaineer. Rock wrens frequent talus slopes and other rocky outcrops which climbers often have to cross on their way to a summit. Dull, gray-brown birds with a buzzy song, rock wrens bounce their rear ends up and down while proclaiming their territory. Because I loved their quirky, perky style, I decided some years ago to locate as many of their nests as was reasonably possible on South Table Mountain, where I have been studying birds for over fifteen years. That field work, in addition to the writing I was doing on birds, finally made me feel like an ornithologist. Forty years late perhaps, but the interest has always been there. Finally, I was doing something useful with it, and something even beyond useful.

3. Two Worlds of Birding

It's a Sunday in mid-May. Wanting to confirm the breeding status of several avian friends, I've decided to explore a favorite marsh in Jefferson County. The riparian canopy boasts mature cottonwoods, tightly bunched around a modest stream. The thick understory so tangles the footing that I must walk up the side of the stream where I have arrived; there is no crossing over.

A wide and rolling grassland surrounds the drainage, incongruous on the periphery of Metropolitan Denver, yet offering the pleasant illusion of seeming to stretch well beyond the reach of the urban giant. Absent the meadowlark, fluting from a blossom of rabbitbrush, and the sparrow, soloing from a slender stalk of mullein, I could be drifting across an ocean—which, in a way, and allowing for the passage of millions of years, I am.

It's the birdsong that has drawn me here. A very attentive vesper sparrow has accompanied me across the grassland, flitting from one perch to another, staying just ahead of me and singing the whole time, until he finally alights in a cottonwood at the edge of the riparian corridor. I suspect he has a nest somewhere out in the grass, and he has deliberately led me over to the creek, in hopes of distracting me away from the nest.

Just behind the sparrow, and directly in front of me now is a plump, inviting wetland that has invaded a sluggish part of stream. It is perfect habitat for the red-winged blackbirds that dance above the cattails, males loudly squawking as they patrol, females sitting attentively, or hiding out of sight. To my right, downstream, two amorous robins chase each other, darting in and out of shrubbery below the cattails, pausing to flirt, then recommencing the chase. To my left, in the cottonwood canopy, I hear warblers and orioles. The memory of such gorgeous creatures invites me to walk upstream, to become hypnotized by seductive glimpses of yellow breasts and orange bellies. Further downstream, flickers trumpet from on high, house wrens reverberate lower down.

I remain riveted before the marsh. This small section of an insignificant stream has captivated me, enveloping my senses, drawing me into itself. My reluctant guide, the vesper sparrow, has now quietly disappeared.

After standing here a while, I notice two strange phenomena. The several habitats surrounding me begin to blur into each other and become one world. Simultaneously, a second world emerges, coextensive with the other, but summoned up by a psychic dimension of topography. The first world, a natural setting, includes the urgent, uncertain business of avian reproduction. The second, mostly a creation of my mind, is full of sound and color, harmoniously composed of water and vegetation, enhanced by dry air and a comfortable temperature, made glorious by solitude and memorable by the sheer unlikeliness that such a place should have escaped development.

The birds seem trapped in one universe, oblivious to mine, though as I watch them I realize how distant my own world is from theirs. I can observe, but I cannot take part. No matter how much I desire to know it, or how I might imagine it, I cannot penetrate the reality of these other creatures' existence.

Chastened by this realization, I focus on a drama unfolding in front of me. Numerous red-wings patrol the cattails at center stage. Behind their noisy chatter, and their restless movement, I detect patterns of order. Males have set up territories, and females congregate around them, often several near one male. Under cover of the male's pyrotechnics, females quietly and cryptically go about nesting. Some are still exploring, but at least one has clearly found her spot: twice I have watched her disappear beside the same stalk, at least once with something in her beak. But I am not the only observer of this scene.

Enter the villain. A female brown-headed cowbird has also been watching. I spotted her when I first stopped at the edge of the stream, while scanning around to identify the locals. For twenty minutes she has been sitting on the limb of a cottonwood on the opposite bank, some forty feet away, watching. I know she has seen the female blackbird plunge toward her nest. If there are eggs on that nest, Mrs. Cowbird will wait until Mrs. Blackbird runs an errand, then descend and quickly deposit her own egg in that nest. The result will be disaster for the blackbirds: cowbird chicks hatch first, are larger and more aggressive, and they destroy the blackbird eggs, or kill the chicks. Tragically, the female blackbird abets this infanticide by nourishing the cowbird chick, apparently unable to distinguish it from her own doomed brood. I watch in rapt anticipation.

When the cowbird finally makes her move, she surprises me. She drops toward the cattails, but veers off to her right, away from the nest I've been watching, and out of sight behind a shrub. Before she has time to do any mischief, her consort appears, eager to mate. She rebuffs him, and both fly off.

Presently, a chilly breeze breaks the spell. For ninety minutes I have been traversing a kind of intergalactic space, between a familiar world and an exotic, alluring one. In thrall to the magic of birds, I have put aside human concerns, have forgotten time, even lost self-consciousness, if only briefly. I'm enriched by an awareness of these temporary disabilities. I want to linger, to learn more, but a kind of cultural gravity is dragging me back. I don't want to go home, but that's where I belong. I don't have a choice, for, every bit as much as the birds, I am trapped by the circumstances of my own world.

4. A Tale of Two Planets

IN THE SPRING OF 2005 I attended a meeting of the Colorado Environmental Coalition, an umbrella group that tries to raise awareness among its many member organizations. I had agreed to be part of a focus group to examine CEC's publications and consider whether any changes were in order. The group began by commending CEC for all the things it was doing right, and our agreement was sincere. After all, we were all dues paying believers. During a break, an attractive young lady named Linda and I continued a conversation we had started on the rapid pace of biological discovery.

I mentioned that from the perspective of someone who had finished college in the late 1950s, we had learned a great deal in a very short time: the double helix structure of DNA (1952), the genetic information encoded in our genes (1964), the discoveries of ecosystems at volcanic vents on the ocean floor (1977) and of ozone holes over Antarctica (1985). We've even cloned a sheep (Dolly, 1996), and itemized the content and structure of the human genome (2003). And those were just samples. As we advance into the twenty-first century, I said, organizations devoted to protecting Nature had many reasons to be proud, even optimistic. We were keeping the public informed of rapid advances in knowledge, and that knowledge (I felt sure) was winning us many new converts.

Linda concurred. "More and more of us have some knowledge of the natural world," she said. "As knowledge grows so does our appreciation and a desire to preserve our natural heritage and quality of life." It was music to my ears to hear her say that "more and more people see that Nature is

17

not an inexhaustible resource, that it can be permanently harmed by the actions of humans." Such realizations have gained such wide currency, she continued with breathless enthusiasm, that surely a huge majority of Americans now wanted to protect Nature. By way of confirmation, she pointed to the various polls and surveys that highlighted the public's growing unanimity on the subject.

At that point I expressed my skepticism about polls. I had not thought through exactly why I found the polls unconvincing, but I said something about old prejudices dying hard. At which point our delightful harmony evaporated in a flash, when Linda said, "The biggest prejudice is the attitude of *your* generation. You guys still want to find enemies. I think environmentalists have moved beyond that and are ready to work with others." Feeling somewhat abashed, and not having a ready response, I scrambled to say something diplomatic and soothing. "Yes," I managed, "We do all have to learn to work together." Incidentally, I don't like the word environmentalist, never have. I prefer the term nature advocate. Protecting Nature while preserving prosperity and enlarging opportunities should be something all humans can learn to agree on.

I went home troubled that Linda might have been right about the old warrior attitudes of the environmental movement. A lot of us had joined the movement because of what we found wrong with the attitude of business, and with the wider philosophy of capitalism itself. We had found enemies. But those enemies were just as convinced that we were wrong, that we were opposing the continued prosperity of America, if not the rest of the world. Some corporations have made efforts to recreate themselves in a greener, more human-oriented image, but have their attitudes gone beyond image? Do they truly understand that all humans and all life share this precious planet, that cooperation must now supersede rivalry, that competition must yield to joint action? The more I thought about it, the more I found reasons to justify my skepticism about whether we are prepared to move forward together.

I think there is a huge but mostly unacknowledged division between nature consumers and nature lovers. Nature consumers approach Nature not on her own terms but with reference to themselves. They see something they want, and they arrange to possess it or use it. Nature is a commodity, to be enjoyed, to be displayed, to be used in ways that enrich us or enhance our own self-image. All of us, including nature lovers, behave as nature consumers at one time or another.

We are not bad people, nature consumers, only addicts. Because America's resources have been plentiful, free enterprise in this country has enjoyed tremendous success. Because technology has transformed our lives, we have become accustomed to convenience, and we now expect a continuous supply of new gadgets and products that delight, stimulate, and educate us. But technology also blinds us to the ominous fact that natural resources are limited, and so is our technology. We cannot have everything.

Nature lovers understand that humans belong to the natural world. We do not stand outside or above Nature, free to use or abuse her without consequence. Everything we do impacts each other, and all other creatures, and all other physical systems on Planet Earth.

But this is a lesson we don't want to learn. We want everything, and we want it now. Our material success has persuaded us that we need have no limits on our expectations. Though we still love Nature, we assume we can bargain with her, we can arrange compromises, we can go on expanding without harming her or ourselves. Thus do we preach the comforting but self-serving homily that ecotourism benefits business and Nature, or that we must extract more oil and gas from wilderness areas, or that oil spills, hazardous waste, and pollution are acceptable tradeoffs for growth. Thus do we sell such nostrums as "sustainability," without acknowledging that we are using up resources faster than we can replace them. And thus do we swallow such nonsense as "smart growth," which becomes an oxymoron every time the most powerful vested interest makes a self-serving decision.

We delude ourselves if we believe such greenwash. Sustainability implies that we use no natural resources faster than we can replace them, and that we can replace them fast enough for current and likely future use. But where is this possible? Nowhere that I know of. Why not? Because vital natural resources—chiefly coal, petroleum, natural gas, quality timber and fresh water—exist in limited amounts. Once depleted, they are gone.

While coal remains abundant, though problematic, petroleum rapidly approaches the bottom of the barrel.

For water, the situation is already dire. Humans now use over half the globally available supply of fresh water; by 2025 hydrologists think we will be using around 70%. Demands for fresh, clean water already outstrip available supply, and surging human populations will only increase the number of those who will have to do with less. At present human uses of water break down as follows, worldwide: 8% for homes, villages, and cities, 22% for industry, and a whopping 70% for agriculture. Consider that one billion human beings today lack even a gallon a day of clean water for drinking and preparing food. That's one out of every six people on the planet. Over one third of the world's people lack safe sanitation systems, which depend on generous amounts of water. Yet in North America we consume more than 150 gallons per person, per day, and that doesn't count our industrial or agricultural uses. To grow enough cotton for a single T-shirt requires over 700 gallons. To produce one pound of beef, over 1,800 gallons; one hamburger, 634 gallons. During the life of one beef cow or steer, a staggering 816,600 gallons of water have been consumed for all purposes related to raising that animal. Just one glass of beer takes 20 gallons, a pound of apples 84 gallons, and one cup of coffee 37 gallons. (See map enclosed with *National Geographic Magazine*, April 2010.) Under these circumstances, imagine the impact of decreasing supplies of water on birds, animals, plants, and all the natural communities.

Planting trees generates a lot of good feeling, because it replaces some of what harvesting takes, but harvesting in the rain forests alone far exceeds any feasible plans for replacement. And what about the even larger realm of the boreal forest? If global warming proceeds at its current pace, this precious resource may be compromised before we learn how to save it.

The only thing smart about growth would be to plan where growth was truly needed. But that would require diverse stakeholders to cooperate in discovering what best served the common good. Instead this country seems driven by narrow interest groups who seek only their own advancement. Planning would require a way of defining the common good, and some political mechanism to ensure that any development went forward in tune with that definition. Given the public's distaste for regulation, and the imagination and private wealth behind lobbyists, how likely is that? Besides, there's money in growth. We have yet to learn how to make money in a steady-state economy. Until all of Pogo's "us" (including those in other countries) begin to place other values above material ones, we will not alter the course of our unsustainable, unintelligent addiction to growth.

Nature does not conform to the hopeful pragmatism of economics. She has her own rules and regulations, starkly opposed to the slick congeniality recently emerged in some quarters, which disdains controversy in favor of consensus. Consensus is fine, but we need to find it, if we can, by obeying Nature's rules, not our own overwrought appetites.

Let us begin by admitting that Americans are the most fortunate people in the history of the Earth (materially speaking), that our good fortune is neither preordained nor secure, that our desires have been excessive, that money and possessions do not equate with happiness, that we can live with less. The yearning for more of everything has delivered lots of stuff but also more anxiety and misery. Pause for a moment to do a quick mental inventory of how many things in your home you don't need. Our periodic garage and rummage sales demonstrate how quickly we tire of the stuff that surrounds us. Why do we assume that more stuff, or different stuff, will brighten our homes or improve our lives? This constant lusting after material goods enables the consumer economy, thus we avoid calling it what it really is: an addiction, on a par with other cravings we pretend to deplore: drugs, sex, work, violence. What does it say about us that we are living from fix to fix?

Accepting sufficiency will reorient us to values deeper than material ones and remind us that true prosperity grows in our hearts and cannot be measured by our financial assets.

5. How Much is Enough?

ALL SPECIES CONTINUALLY EVOLVE, SPREADING and contracting in range, increasing and shrinking in abundance, assuming new traits and shedding others. All this happens so slowly that we tend to take it for granted, if we even notice it, so that the causes of one species flourishing and another languishing are sufficiently complex that most of us ignore them.

Left to itself, Nature tends over time to balance out the ups and downs that alternately impel and imperil all living creatures. But, due to the nearly ubiquitous footprint of humankind, Nature is no longer left to itself. Because of our arrogance regarding Nature, and our ignorance of natural processes, our impacts almost always create harm. Our craving for material growth is eroding the natural systems which sustain life itself. Such an astonishing irony should be intolerable to intelligent beings.

> *The one process ongoing . . . that will take millions of years*
> *to correct is the loss of genetic and species diversity*
> *by the destruction of natural habitats. This is the folly*
> *our descendants are least likely to forgive us.*
> Edward O. Wilson

But intelligence and appetite are often good buddies. We manufacture, circulate, and consume an enormous variety of stuff, way more than we need, much of it designed for one-time use. As a result in the United States alone we generate 210 million tons of trash annually. We recycle some 27% of that. Except for food scraps and yard waste, most of what winds up in landfills (paper, wood products, plastics, metals, glass, rubber and leather) could be recycled, but isn't, which reflects the unsustainable throwaway mentality symptomatic among developed countries.

> *We who prayed and wept*
> *for liberty from kings*
> *and the yoke of liberty*
> *accept the tyranny of things*
> *we do not need.*
> *In plenitude too free,*
> *we have become adept*
> *beneath the yoke of greed.*
> Wendell Berry

Two pathologies seem to accompany increasing consumption. First, the distinction between genuine needs and frivolous wants becomes blurred: what one wants becomes a need.

> *Confirm thy soul in self-control.*
> America the Beautiful

Second, the more one accumulates, the more one becomes possessive, hungry for more, and insecure about keeping what one has—the results being apparent in the disparity of wealth among individuals and between nations.

> *Excess of wealth is cause of covetousness.*
> Christopher Marlowe

The more we get, the less we seem to care about other people, other creatures, or the public good.

> *Selfishness is the greatest curse of the human race.*
> William Gladstone

Contrast this cruel narrowness with the confident inclusiveness of the Enlightenment, when European and American leaders (among them, our Founding Fathers) crafted the first universal perspective on mankind. Its aim was to alter the destiny of humanity by employing more reason and less authority.

> *Enlighten the people generally, and tyranny and oppression*
> *of body and mind will vanish like evil spirits at the dawn of day.*
> Thomas Jefferson

Our own Benjamin Franklin epitomized the versatility of these leaders, whose watchword was public service. We mostly remember Franklin as a statesman, a diplomat, a shrewd politician, a prolific essayist—and a lady's man. But he was so much more. Franklin became rich as an entrepreneurial printer, but he generously shared his business acumen with scores of others. He organized an insurance company, a hospital, a library, a university, and Pennsylvania's first effective militia.

No personal considerations should stand in the way
of performing a public duty.
Ulysses S. Grant

Idealistic yet practical, Franklin and his colleagues remind us that the health and prosperity of a nation are measured by the willingness of its citizens to contribute to the common good.

Ask not what your country can do for you,
but what can you do for your country?
John F. Kennedy

Now we must learn to think beyond the narrow confines of our own countries. We must rediscover the wider world, and our place in it.

Our task must be to free ourselves . . . by widening
our circle of compassion to embrace all living
creatures and the whole of Nature and its beauty.
Albert Einstein

Not such a difficult task, really, once we acknowledge (or remember) that we humans share genetic material with all living things. Consider: the cells in our bodies contain numerous organelles, each with specialized functions, and our DNA is enclosed in a membrane-bound nucleus. This is the eukaryotic cell, and it evolved at least 1.2 billion years ago. It is characteristic of all animals, plants, fungi, and some really strange critters known as protistans, which means that we share the same cell structure with everything that lives, except blue green algae and bacteria. We share some genes with all living things, more with those closest to us on the tree of life, like the great apes (c. 98%), but also a certain amount with sponges, lobsters, insects, and all those weird invertebrates, even with blue green algae and bacteria. That so many living forms of life share the same cell structure, and varying proportions of the same genes, nicely demonstrates the connectedness of species through evolution. It is sobering to remember, too, that even inanimate matter consists of the same atoms, compounds, and molecules as ourselves, and are subject to the same laws of physics and chemistry.

We are Nature, long have we been absent, but now we return.
Walt Whitman

It is a remembering we need, not a brainwashing or a cultural reprograming. The ancients knew most of what we now need to know about humankind, its problems and possibilities, its mores and its morals, its exultations and its execrable deeds. The ancients learned the flimsiness of individual power, the strength of cooperation, the immensity of appetite, the dangers of excess, and the wisdom of sufficiency.

Enough is as good as a feast.
Book of Proverbs

I don't mean to imply that the ancients behaved any better than we do today. Corruption, greed, violence, selfishness, shortsightedness, even evil have always been with us. It's a matter of balance. When we forget our connectedness, we lose our way, and the mindless beasts dominate and plunder us. When we remember our better selves, we keep the beasts at bay. May the remembering begin.

6. South Table Mountain: Winter

DECEMBER 26: A FIERCELY COLD and blustery day. What am I doing here? Call me crazy, but I've come here in terrible conditions to observe in person the survival skills of my four-legged and winged friends. Not so crazy. Makes me appreciate the comforts of home, the resilience of life, its gripping tenacity. As I grow softer and more comfortable, also more stale and stupid, I need to remember our origins in the wild. To draw strength from our animal relatives. Plodding around like this on a cold wintry day may seem foolish, but it puts me in touch with the elements that have blended so intimately with human history. There's a deep satisfaction in doing so, far more impactive than the temporary discomfort I experience.

South Table Mountain (STM) is a mesa that rises above and just to the east of the town of Golden, Colorado. It is a prominent landmark, so much so that its high point, Castle Rock, a thick neck of volcanic rock thrusting up to an abrupt climax at 6,319 feet, has become the symbol and logo for the City of Golden, above which it rises like a protective tower. Despite this vertical prominence, the mesa gives no hint from any viewpoint below of its three-and-a-half square mile area, which can only be appreciated by wandering around the grasslands on top and exploring the shrubs that clothe its flanks on all sides. Nor would even an experienced birder guess that well over a hundred different avian species either dwell or visit here every year.

Clear Creek flows past the north side of STM. One of the numerous streams draining the foothills to the west, its waters pass through

Metropolitan Denver before moving east to nourish the plains. Just to the north of Clear Creek is STM's twin, North Table Mountain. Long ago the twins formed part of an unbroken section of the familiar country rock nearby. Then Clear Creek got to work gouging and scraping and tearing at that hunk of rock, until it created a valley between them and two separate hunks. Both mesas have essentially the same geology and habitats. Paleozoic sandstones support the mesas, both of which consist of volcanic tuff of late Cretaceous and early Tertiary age called The Denver Formation; three lava flows of latite (basalt) are interbedded with the Tertiary portion. This geographic setting boasts two famous features, each attracting its own group of tourists. The first is the K-T Boundary, separating the Mesozoic and Cenozoic eras and bespeaking the end of the dinosaurs. The other is Coors Brewery, an agglomeration straddling the banks of Clear Creek, neatly confined between the two mesas.

I hike up an old animal trail on the north slope of STM, through shrubs and across a spring that waters a small riparian habitat. Despite the similarity of the two mesas, I'm partial to STM. I used to live just beneath it. A great horned owl roosted in a locust tree of the front yard, but he had a nest in the cliffs of STM, where he and his mate raised several broods. For over fifteen years I have been walking up, over, and around this splendid mesa, in all seasons, mostly looking for those numerous birds. A variety of shrubs house and protect and feed the impressive avian diversity; shrubs dominate the slopes and extend up to the edges of the grassland on top. Little disturbance exists along the slopes, so shrubs become the climax community. The most common are wild plum, chokecherry, and mountain mahogany. On the cooler northern slopes are skunkbrush, wax current, and rabbitbrush.

The trail I follow begins at around 5,600 feet and heads west through the shrubs to reach the grasslands, then turns south just a smidgen, then east briefly to reach the high point of the mesa's center. My map measures this knoll at 6,142 feet, from which I have a good view of the whole mountain. Its overall shape suggests an oval, but one snipped with numerous gullies and valleys and disfigured with a large north-trending bulge, making it resemble, from an aerial view, a primitive fish sporting a prominent dorsal fin.

Striding northwest from the knoll, I head for the shrubs at the edge of the mesa, hoping to scare up some birds. Birds are always here, but it becomes more difficult to ferret them out in stormy weather. Many will be hiding in the shrubs, out of the wind, or down on the ground where piles of seeds have accumulated. No birdsong breaks the silence. No scurrying gives away the position of small rodents or mammals. All is still. Finally, after standing just inside the shrubs for what seems a long time, I am rewarded by a flock of American tree sparrows. I count eight. They have been down on the ground, probably foraging, and half of them arise in unison to the upper branches of the shrubs, where they have an unobstructed view of me. The other four follow separately in short order behind the others. Not a peep do they utter. These denizens of arctic lands only visit Colorado in the dead of winter. They enjoy cold weather and remind me how wonderfully adapted birds can be, to all seasons and nearly all habitats. Satisfied that I intend them no harm, and after a dignified interval, they fly down slope and disappear in another clump of shrubs.

Looking down at the northern slope of the mesa, I am reminded that human impact here has declined over the past century. Gone are the cattle that arrived with the first settlers. Gone are the gravel quarries that flourished from the 1930s into the 1950s. Gone is the Table Mountain Gun Club that existed in Quarry 4 until around 1966, when the Rolling Hills Country Club opened just to the north of the mesa.

Standing on the slope among the shrubs, I have been partially shielded from the wind. Just as I am about ready to head back up hill, I notice the swooping, dipping, rolling form of a northern harrier, better known as the marsh hawk. A crow-sized raptor with a distinctive white rump patch, the harrier looks like it might be a cross between a kite and a falcon, though it is neither. It belongs to a genus all its own. This skillful hunter disguises its fierce nature by exuding nonchalance. With wings often slightly raised in a V-shape, this may be the most versatile and agile flyer ever to take to the air. Deliberate, poised, alert, and simultaneously powerful, intrepid, yet mostly invisible to the prey it hunts so patiently, so astutely, so relentlessly. Watching its lilting, buoyant flight pattern becomes hypnotic, and likely it lulls and beguiles the unwary rabbit or vole or mouse or frog or snake or small bird or even the unlucky magpie, upon which it can drop like a thunderbolt without warning. Yet this matchless bird can soar like a hawk or glide like an eagle. This particular bird is a juvenile with an orange front and a dark back. He patrols the border between grassland and shrub. He seems indifferent to the cold and the biting wind. I am not, so I move on.

I walk back to the knoll, intending to continue south in order to inspect the shrubs at the southern edge of the mesa. Looking west from the knoll, I recall that a tourist facility sprang up on the western end of the mesa, beginning in 1906, which eventually included a café, dance hall, lighthouse, and a funicular built to Castle Rock in 1913. Fire destroyed the resort in 1927. On this western side a power line runs north-south across and beyond the mesa, suspended from seven huge towers, a solitary and silent reminder of mankind. Though the towers spoil somewhat the view of the foothills and Front Range, they provide excellent roosts for raptors. Golden eagles and big hawks regularly take possession of them.

No eagles today. But I hear the familiar squawk of a black-billed magpie. He (she?) flaps up over the same slope I just ascended and now heads toward a former rock quarry. Looking for grubs or any small thing that moves. This bird eats anything and everything, including eggs of other birds and their chicks, hence its nasty reputation. But this bird makes a home in most habitats and belongs to a family, the corvids, that inhabits every continent of the Earth except Antarctica. Magpies are smart, adaptable, gregarious, and gorgeous. Distinctive are the long tail and the level, somewhat labored flight pattern. This tuxedo-clad cousin of jays and crows is striking in his year-round pied plumage, set off by iridescent flashes of bluish green.

To the south and slightly east from the knoll, a paved highway warps itself into a giant triangle, a pursuit-training course for the Colorado Highway Patrol—a rural-looking but rude intrusion onto the grasslands atop the mesa, which remain the realm of rodents, deer, birds, and insects. Surrounding the pursuit course are dozens of poles, apparently tossed as spears by some giant huntress in a bygone age and for a reason now forgotten. Wires connect the poles, but for no obvious contemporary purpose. But the poles attract raptors in every season, especially red-tailed hawks. Today I spy only one. He twists his head some ninety degrees to look me over, then twists back toward the grasslands beyond. He awaits the appearance of breakfast.

Just behind the pursuit course is the only building atop the mountain, a sprawling portion of the Department of Energy's National Renewable Energy Laboratory. It arose shortly after DOE acquired lands on the mesa from Camp George West in 1977; an additional portion of NREL reposes at the base of the southern slope. Visually, the pursuit course and NREL seem out of place. Yet, unburdened with my refined esthetics, the wildlife treat even this portion of the mesa as home. Rabbits scurry everywhere. Elsewhere on the mesa coyotes and foxes den, as do prairie dogs and burrowing owls. Friends who live beneath the mesa report that mountain lions have been seen here; black bear prowl the nearby foothills and may also have discovered this near wilderness oasis in the city.

On days like today I am reminded of a favorite relative, Uncle Henry Roberts, after whom I named my son. Uncle Hank used to say that, after December 21—the day of the winter solstice, when the Earth gradually begins to tilt the northern hemisphere back toward the warming rays of the sun—the back of winter is broken. It was typical of Uncle Hank to see the larger, hidden gyrations behind the daily cycles of our existence. His insight provides some comfort on a day so cold that I don't dare stand still for long. For those of us not able to hibernate or migrate, movement equals survival.

During winter on STM I often think of Uncle Hank for another reason. Shortly before dying of cancer, he said, "Death is no big deal. It's only Nature's way of saying 'slow down'." The pithy stoicism was typical of this wonderful man, as was the subtle, abnegating humor. I have often recalled with admiration his brave assessment of the endgame, but today I am reminded of a different insight of his wise words, an insight that epitomizes winter. Winter is the time of slowing down. It is the season, the only season, when all the natural elements and forces surrounding us conspire to slacken our stride.

We humans don't take such restrictions kindly. Mostly we define ourselves by our achievements, but winter thwarts us with formidable roadblocks. I have been up here in blizzards so thick I could barely see ten feet ahead. I have slogged through snow deep enough to discourage all but the shortest hikes. Winter here is magnificent, not least because it reminds me to adjust my psyche to the seasons, to discover again how to learn just by being alert, how to progress by holding still. For Nature and all her creatures, including us, winter is a time of rest, of renewal. Humans rest and renew rather differently than animals and plants. Unlike rabbits or rabbitbrush, we remember and anticipate. No doubt rabbits cogitate and plan, in their own way—perhaps even rabbitbrush, at a level we do not understand—but it matters little to us whether they do or not. It matters that we reflect, and winter is the ideal time for reflection. Philosophers may debate which between reflection and activity is the obverse or reverse side of the human coin, but they are conjoined. My sense is that we could all use more reflection and less activity.

So what goes through my mind on this bitter cold day? I'm thinking that the top of a windblown mesa compares poorly to my warm study at home as a place for philosophic inquiry! But mostly, I find myself thinking about thought. The logical deployment of ideas, like the steady march of soldiers, marshals only an aspect of thought, just as the rude and sometimes dangerous bursts of irrationality only amount to the sniper fire of thought. Flashes of insight and flights of imagination disdain the vulgar battlefields of the mind: such inspirations come from our muses. Those spirits inhabit the ethereal realm beyond our beck and call, and it amuses them to combine samples of our experience with a slice of our desires and to package these volatile elements into thunderbolts, which they hurl at us during unsuspecting moments—in the shower, at the theatre, driving to an urgent appointment, lying abed not wanting to stir, moaning in the depths of despair, or groaning in the heat of passion.

Jolted back to reality by snowdrift that scours my face, I remember the last time I walked this particular route, around the central part of the mountain, skirting the western edge of the pursuit course. It was last spring, when I remember finding over thirty different bird species. Today, so far, I have found only a handful. In winter, fifteen is a good count; ten is the norm.

During summer, when the gorgeous neo-tropical birds pass through, or stay to breed, many species will specialize in a particular habitat. Not in winter. Resources are too scarce in any location, so the winter residents tend to be generalists. American tree sparrows and house finches prefer shrubs, but I'll more often find them around the houses that ring the base of the mesa. Even western scrub jays explore beyond their namesake habitat in winter, as do spotted towhees. Handouts from feeders become crucial for all species in winter here, especially the specialists. The same is true of mammals. At night deer shamelessly explore the streets where houses nestle to find the tastiest buds in gardens. Even elk have been known to appear here in winter. Bears invade bird feeders. Rabbits become as common as house pets. Only the coyote seems to have the dignity, and the hunting skill, to disdain free food—unless you count backyard pets left outside at night.

An extraordinary bird often rewards my winter wanderings: here is the northern shrike, a favorite winter resident, who shows up even during stormy days. The same one (I think) has returned for several winters in a row. I make that identification with some confidence, because I often find him in the same cottonwood, which stands apart from others huddled together in a well-watered gully. From his solitary perch, as from the icy mast of a ship, the shrike commands a sweeping view of the frozen grasslands. Despite my approaching in a circuitous manner, and making every effort not to appear threatening, the shrike usually takes wing before I arrive at the base of his tree. But once he allowed me to pass directly underneath, without fleeing. It was a magical moment. I like to think he recognized me.

Prairie falcons are another reward. They live here year round, but my favorite memory is a wintry one. One day while striding along at a good clip, trying to stay warm, I caused some unease in the shrubs along the edge of the mesa. I saw a couple of rabbits scurry for safer cover, but paid them little attention, when suddenly the falcon zoomed overhead and dropped near some creature. I realized the falcon had been using me as a beater, to scare up game. I continued at a fast pace, trying to oblige the bird by heading into the heart of the thicket.

Mostly what I find in winter are the hearty year-round residents: magpies, crows, flickers, starlings, doves, towhees, house sparrows, house finches, black-capped chickadees, and the few lingering blue jays. In winter they are joined by mountain chickadees, juncos, the odd Steller's jay down from the mountains, those ever-surprising robins, who turn up in flocks, and, once in a while, a white-breasted nuthatch, the only one of its genus to visit in winter. Townsend's solitaires winter here because of the urban setting at the base of the mesa, where they find juniper berries, their preferred winter food. Canyon wrens remain in the cliffs but rarely sing. When they do sing, their cascading music is both the most haunting and the most thrilling of sounds. Song sparrows stay until December, white-crowned sparrows sometimes until late January. Every winter brings a truly surprising bird: one year it was the hermit thrush passing through in early December. Another year it was five eastern bluebirds in late November.

And, of course, the raptors. A pair of great horned owls have nested in the cliffs for as long as I have been coming here. Golden eagles remain over winter, as do red-tailed hawks, American kestrels, and prairie falcons. Northern harriers pass through, and take their time doing so. One hangs around for most of the cold season, more years than not. The rough-legged hawk comes here only in winter, but I have only a few records: are they just more cryptic than other raptors, or do most rough-legs choose a different nearby habitat? These denizens of the arctic tend to use the same niches recently vacated by Swainson's hawks, who spend their winters in Argentina.

The one species I don't find much in winter is *Homo sapiens*. Few bikers. Few hikers. Few joggers. Rarely someone walking their dog. Most of the time I am the only human in sight, at least during week days, and for sure during storms.

When not stormy or frightfully cold, STM can be quite serene in winter. February is often a hopeful child, caught between feuding parents. The sudden, swirling ballerinas of December are past. The invasion of soggy, sullen paratroopers is still to come in March. The accumulated blanket of snow smoothes out little lumps and bumps in the land, hides water at the bottom of draws, and protects sleeping creatures beneath its insulating warmth. Depositing itself so uniformly up the slopes and across the flats, snow hides more than it reveals. But the abundance and diversity of life remain. Beneath the frozen surface of the grassland, and holding fast to the stiff branches of shrubs and trees are millions, perhaps billions, of eggs and seeds and larvae. Countless microbes constantly shift the soil, working unobtrusively, remembering nothing, anticipating nothing.

On such a day, the mesa seems completely isolated. The air holds itself utterly still, the sky sparkles a brittle blue. My boots provide a satisfying crunch with each step, at times the only sound across this silent land. I might as well be traipsing along the back side of the Moon. Though surrounded by Metro Denver, STM is high enough and extensive enough to exclude, from many spots, a view of anything but another part of itself. The mesa is a secret enclave of small hollows and channels, dens and sinks, which deny the urban behemoth below and muffle its unnatural noises.

I find my friend the shrike. I also see the owl briefly, flying from his cave. He and his mate may be incubating eggs by now. A blue jay scolds me as I pass "his" garden. Or was he saluting me? Altogether I find sixteen species, quite a lot for the season. Because of the warm day and the welcome activity of birds, I am able to slow down as I walk across the sleeping land, to pause and look, to reflect and wonder. I drink in the silence, wonder at the diversity of hidden life, and ponder my own renewal.

Precisely because they now hide out of sight, I am keenly aware of my tie with all the creatures who live here, and I reflect how these precious few connect to others across the region and around the globe. We cannot afford to lose any of them, for we are part of them, and they of us. This awareness is both an ecological lesson and a spiritual insight, and it has nourished humans since our first appearance as a species. Now it can restore the balance in our souls—if only we would let it.

7. Plumbing and Virtue

Bᴀᴄᴋ ᴏɴ 18 Jᴜɴᴇ 2004 I took part in another fruitful meeting, this one the inaugural meeting of the Colorado Council of The Nature Conservancy. Participants discussed whether the needs for water could be balanced between the natural and the human communities.

Let's begin by recognizing that water use is already way out of balance. Nature provides all water, for both the natural and human communities, and it makes possible most uses through a complex system known as the water cycle. Humans provide no water, but our advanced technological abilities enable us to exercise an increasing influence over most uses. As we continue to find new ways to exert that influence, we have yet to acknowledge our stewardship over water for other "customers" in the natural communities. In other words, so far our ability has outrun our responsibility. Perhaps it is time to remember that our abilities only evolved over time, and because of resources provided by Nature, chief among them water.

In the long view of evolution human interference with Nature would probably not have become threatening, if humans had not invented agriculture around 11,000 years ago. With more food and settled communities those first farmers revolutionized shelter, health, security, and how they thought. Civilization as we know it was on its way, complete with religion, art, philosophy, government, wealth, travel, and—finally!—miniskirts and football.

Those early farmers not only changed the course of history, they also influenced every generation of humans since their time, including ours. They invented a lifestyle that lengthened our lives, increased our opportunities, and essentially made possible the attractive and dangerous species we have become. Along the way those early farmers pioneered an enjoyment of leisure, a fascination with more and more things to amuse and challenge us, and a desire for comfort.

But comfort has consequences. One of them is that yesterday's luxuries become today's necessities without anyone ever stopping to ask, "Do I really need or even want that?" "That" could be our preference, even in the semiarid West, for lawns over natural landscaping, or our growing love affair with golf courses, or the provision in all modern homes of multiple bathrooms. I grew up in a household of four children and two adults, who shared two bathrooms. My experience is not unusual.

Humans now use over half the globally available supply of fresh water. Consider just one aspect of our industrial uses of water. Almost everything manufactured requires water at some stage of the process, and most manufacturing depends on electricity, which we generate mostly by burning fossil fuels or by building hydroelectric plants. Recently, we have learned the downside of burning coal and natural gas, but dams present massive problems too. Much of the water dams capture evaporates; they impede the natural flows of water and sediment on which animals and plants depend; they prevent the migration of many aquatic species; their turbines kill some species; they concentrate pollutants; and eventually they all silt up. The concentration of water and sediment behind dams creates an extremely heavy mass—often in the millions of tons for large dams—that frequently triggers nearby earthquakes. Imagine the devastation should an earthquake damage one of the large dams along the Colorado River. Dams are a classic symbol of frantic civilizations, drunk with technological prowess, impatient to "control" Nature, and blind to the implications of their muscular haste.

Don't get me wrong: I'm no Luddite. Given the choices we have made, we can no longer live without electricity and some of the many consumer products it makes possible, like computers, but all of them are produced with lots of water. Many of them cater to style and amusement but don't fill any real needs. Do we need a new cell phone every six months? Does every child require a laptop? How many electronic toys are required to produce happiness?

Isn't it time that we remembered the distinction between sufficiency and abundance? Nothing wrong with a feast once in a while, when the occasion warrants one. But a perpetual orgy perverts the appetite, just as any insatiable hunger for the ultimate destroys our ability to appreciate the ordinary events of life. Restraint is more than common sense; it is also a virtue. And virtue depends on a system of ethics.

But what do virtue and ethics have to do with water resources? Actually, quite a lot. Because one billion human beings lack even a gallon a day of clean water for drinking and preparing food, while in North America we consume more than 150 gallons per person, per day, we have a moral issue on our hands. What does it say about our priorities in America that xeriscaping commands so little attention? What does it say about our intelligence that we treat water more as a commodity (selling it in designer brands) than as a precious, limited resource? What does it say of our awareness that we blandly draw down water supplies but do very little about conservation, repairing leaks, building more efficient appliances, or eliminating wasteful practices?

So it seems we do need virtue and ethics. And to reconnect with them, we need Aristotle. Aristotle (384-322 B.C.) was one of those brilliant polymaths who could synthesize several fields at once, and draw from them a common essence. He wrote of the sciences and the humanities before those disciplines became separated by specialization. He looked beyond facts to find patterns. He understood that in the life sciences unity and diversity were parts of a single process. He has influenced every division of the modern curriculum, including ethics.

Aristotle taught what I call a deep morality. He reasoned that human behavior conformed to certain principles, principles similar to those governing Nature, and that these principles influenced each other, were parts of a larger whole. For example, politics and ethics have in common the goal of achieving human happiness. (Pause to let that one sink in!) Once you have digested that astonishing proposition, the goals of philosophy, economics, psychology, art, etc. prove to be much the same. Aristotle excelled at applying reason, and he argued that man was a rational animal, capable of harnessing various stallions to pull the same chariot and directing them toward the same goal. Thanks to the science of ecology, which demonstrates connections, we are rediscovering the wisdom of Aristotle.

By the way, Aristotle never said that man was completely rational. To the contrary, he emphasized that acting rationally was a learned behavior, one that countered or channeled the irrational force of passions. Ethics for Aristotle—his deep morality—consisted of a series of rational choices, choices that a welter of irrational desires opposed, but which enabled him to find a path for life analogous to the course of a ship through a stormy sea.

The obsession in America with consuming, and the assertion of numerous "rights" to do whatever we want, raise doubts about this country's ability to balance the needs of mankind with those of Nature. Worse, our wasteful depletion of natural resources, water in particular, raises doubts about our basic humanity. To borrow a phrase from Abraham Lincoln, we are now engaged in a contest to determine "whether that nation, or any nation so conceived and so dedicated, can long endure."

The answer depends on intelligence, which in turn depends on choices, choices based on deep morality. Many Americans are capable, educated, informed, idealistic, and energetic. Yet most of us are yoked to our electronic devices, our fuelish cars, our green lawns, and more stuff than we need, or, I would wager, more than we really want. We all endorse implicitly an economic system that has put the Earth in peril today, because mankind's relentless quest for more comfort, more leisure, and more wealth endangers the natural resources on which those benefits depend. Those benefits are part of what Aristotle included in happiness, but Aristotle also counseled moderation. Is it too late for Americans, so habituated to excess, to relearn moderation?

8. The Change That Will Not Wait

Wʀɪᴛɪɴɢ ᴀ sʜᴏʀᴛ ᴇssᴀʏ ᴏɴ climate change may be about as effective as spraying an angry rhinoceros with a water gun. Still, a raging rhino is an apt metaphor for the widespread and devastating effects of global warming, the most awesome and dangerous aspect of climate change. World leaders still fail to grasp the menace in the beast. Before the Copenhagen Conference in December 2009, expectations were that world leaders would craft comprehensive tactics for dealing with climate change, and embrace binding resolutions to limit carbon emissions. That they accomplished neither goal must give every thoughtful citizen on the planet cause to wonder whether the world's political leaders—so divided by nationalistic hubris and partisan politics—have lost the will to cooperate on matters that impact all of us.

Of course, leaders will not move until citizens push them, and many citizens are not pushing because they are confused about global warming. They hear the figures about increasing temperatures, but they still shiver in winter, and their cars still get stuck in snowdrifts. So let's begin by distinguishing climate from weather. Weather is what happens each day, and it can change from day to day, season to season, and year to year. Climate is the long-term trend in which weather is heading. Daily weather is comparable to the ups and downs in an individual life, like getting married, or losing a job, or becoming a grandparent. Climate is analogous to broader historical shifts, which gradually impact many individuals over long periods of time. Think of all the people who have been moving from farms to cities over hundreds of years and how many changes that migration has caused in millions of lives. Long-term changes in the climate are not discernible if you are only watching the daily or seasonal weather, but short-term alterations in the weather can hint at larger shifts in the climate. For example, climate scientists predict that because of global warming, fluctuations in weather will become more severe and will upset traditional patterns in regions all across the globe.

The climate of Planet Earth is changing, and there is no longer any doubt about the impact of global warming. What remains controversial is how much of it humans are causing. But first things first. Let's start by summarizing the damage caused by that raging rhino.

Decreasing supply of fresh water

Glaciers and ice sheets are receding in the vicinity of both poles, and in all mountain ranges. The Columbia Glacier, for example, in western Alaska has receded ten miles in the last thirty years. It now retreats a half mile a year, which is eight times faster than thirty years ago. In a recent year forty billion tons of ice moved down the fjord of the Jakobshavn Glacier in western Greenland and into the sea. This is way more than is being replaced by new snow, and the same is true of receding polar ice shelves and sea ice. These chilling facts were reported in "Extreme Ice," a program on PBS's *Nova* that aired in March 2009. Some scientists estimate that we have already lost forty percent of the Arctic ice cap.

To put such losses into perspective, only two to three percent of all the water on Earth is fresh water, which we and all land-dwelling species depend upon for drinking. Not to mention growing crops, washing, sanitation, and assorted industrial uses. Water locked up in glaciers, sea ice, and ice sheets is fresh water. It is, or has been, an essential reserve for all terrestrial life. But the amount of fresh water on the planet is fixed. We can't create more of it. Yet the needs for it are growing dramatically: the world's population exploded from one to six billion during the last century. The next time you find yourself wasting water, imagine the prospect of water wars between nations, even between the "producing" states like Colorado and the "consuming" states like California. Given the fixed amount and the increasing demand, water wars seem a likely scenario of our future, unless we get serious about conservation.

Some folks, not easily alarmed, claim that we have vast reserves of underground water in aquifers. One of the world's largest exists beneath eight breadbasket states here in America, where we do most of our farming. This Ogallala Aquifer covers around 174,000 square miles. That should add up to a lot of water, but while the Ogallala Aquifer has been filling for several million years, in the last 150 years we have been depleting it rapidly with intensive agriculture, much faster than it can recharge. Yes, there are other aquifers, notably those in the MacKenzie River Basin of Oregon, but once we start "mining" them, each will deplete faster than they can recharge.

Other not-easily-ruffled folk talk about desalinization of the oceans, to provide a limitless source of fresh water. This is a typical dream of those who assume technology will solve all our difficulties, but there are a couple of little problems. Desalinization is not yet feasible on the required scale; it may never be. Even if it were, desalinization leaves concentrated salts behind, which become a toxic waste and may harm fresh water supplies. Sixteen billion gallons of fresh water are currently being produced daily by the world's 14,450 desalinization plants. Compared to the vast oceans, that is a mere drop in the bucket, but accelerating production at some point will destabilize ocean and shoreline ecosystems and threaten creatures living in the oceans, which will ultimately threaten us, because we depend in many ways on oceans remaining in a stable condition.

Decreasing food resources

As Antarctic ice shelves diminish, so do the number of krill that grow there, with direct impacts on creatures like penguins and whales, and indirect impacts on the whole food chain that depends on this basic food source. Imagine having less fish to eat. Imagine life without sushi bars. What would all the Catholics eat on Friday?

As the oceans absorb greenhouse gases, not only do they warm but they become more acidic. More acidic oceans make it difficult for mollusks, crustaceans, and corals to make the shells which protect them. Nearly half of the U. S. seafood catch—46%— includes such creatures. Do you like eating crab or shrimp or lobster? Imagine those creatures disappearing:

they are headed in that direction. Increasing oceanic acidity also decreases the productivity of phytoplankton, the tiny photosynthetic plants that make possible the oceanic food web, and provide the planet with half its oxygen. Imagine our planet with only half the oxygen. Would that not alter the chemical balance of gases in the atmosphere? Might that become unhealthy for creatures dependent upon oxygen?

As climate changes around the globe all crop lands, range lands, and cultivated areas where we grow food will be impacted. Disruptions will occur in harvesting, distributing, and bringing food to market. Ironically, some regions will become better suited to agriculture than before, but these will include areas of forest, shrubland, or grassland, some of them in wilderness areas or national reserves, that cannot be plowed without accelerating losses of biodiversity. At the moment Americans are fortunate to be able to argue over the virtues of processed versus organic foods. Imagine having less of both. Want to think about food wars?

Also the balance among plants is shifting, away from sedges and forbs favored by wildlife, toward shrubs and grasses, which kill off the lichen and mosses that support greater biodiversity. Biodiversity directly supports human health and happiness.

Flooding, storms, disease, instability

Rising sea levels have already created a host of interrelated problems in places as diverse as island nations (e.g., Tuvalu, Kiribati, the Maldives, and the Marshall Islands), Bangladesh (90% of which is flood plain), The Netherlands, Venice, London, villages and hunting grounds of the Inuit and Iñupiaq peoples in the Arctic, and, closer to home, the Everglades, the city of Miami, Cape Hatteras, Delaware and Chesapeake Bays.

At the same time, all oceans are warming, and sea levels are rising as warm water expands. Influx of fresh water from receding glaciers and melting ice adds to rising sea levels. What's going to happen to your beachfront home?

Besides the obvious losses of human property, more subtle results are the salinization of water supplies, loss of tidal pools, mangroves, salt marshes and other habitats near shorelines. Does that matter to you? It does if you depend on fresh water. Global warming is implicated in the outbreak of fungi that kill amphibians, and in the dramatic increases in malaria, Dengue fever, hantavirus, and West Nile virus. Research suggests that similar microbes multiplied during four of the five previous mass extinctions of life on the planet, each of which was accompanied by rising temperatures.

From such fertile ground grow social disorder, displaced people, economic disruption, insecurity, and war—all due to greater needs but declining resources. The same point was recently made in a lead story of 9 August 2009 in *The New York Times*, entitled "Climate Change Seen as Threat to U.S. Security."

Severe impacts in the American West

In March 2008 The Rocky Mountain Climate Organization and the Natural Resources Defense Council issued an important report, *Hotter and Drier: The West's Changed Climate*. Here are some of the facts.

The eleven states of the American Far West have been hit harder than any of the lower forty-eight by global warming. The average temperature of the planet rose one degree Fahrenheit during the twentieth century. In the West it rose 1.7 degrees. That means the West, already dry, has been getting drier, and will only continue to get drier. A drier West will be a more challenging place for wildlife to find food resources, water, and suitable habitat, all of which are expected to shrink. A drier West will be a more expensive, more challenging place for humans too. Water has always been scarce in this region. Over the previous century snowfall has been decreasing, so the snowpack is shrinking—again a long term trend, not contradicted by exceptional years of snowy weather. The snow melts earlier in the spring, thus less water is available when most wanted, in summer. More rain now falls during winter, and that rain melts snow and causes flooding. And less snow means less skiing, at least less quality skiing that westerners, and the many vacationers who visit the region, have learned to expect.

Lake Powell, created behind the Glen Canyon Dam on the Colorado River for water storage, dropped by two-thirds between 2000 and 2005. It and Lake Mead, behind the Hoover Dam, are both holding only about 50% of their capacity.

Within the next five years some biologists think that mountain pine beetles will destroy all mature lodgepole pine forests. Because low temperatures in winter are no longer prolonged, more beetles survive the cold season. As a result, beetles are extending their range into higher latitudes and higher elevations. They now threaten bristlecone and limber pines. In the Yellowstone area beetles now destroy the whitebark pines, the seeds of which are a chief food for grizzly bears. Aspen trees are declining across the West. Piñon pines are retreating in the Four Corners area. Do you enjoy forest vistas? Do you like or depend upon wood products? After insects and loggers have decimated the forests, imagine our national parks becoming tiny forest museums.

Increased drought causes more numerous and more intense wildfires, cutting dry land harvest production, slicing income from livestock, and placing many animal and plant species at greater risk. Among those at risk are trout in those famous Montana rivers, and salmon in California's Klamath River.

Among my avian friends in Colorado whose habitats are declining, partly due to global warming, are the bobolink, sharp-tailed grouse, and a bird that was only recently discovered as a separate species, the Gunnison sage-grouse. Other birds whose habitats are shrinking across the West include the northern pintail, green-winged teal, whooping crane, lesser nighthawk, black swift, and eastern meadowlark.

It's all connected

Twenty-five percent of the Northern Hemisphere consists of frozen soil (permafrost) that is gradually melting, causing release of more CO_2 and methane (an even more powerful greenhouse gas than CO_2), with added impacts on climate change. Yes, because of warming, more plants are growing, and plants absorb CO_2, but the decomposition of organic matter in the permafrost is proceeding faster, resulting in a net gain of greenhouse gases.

Because of warming, the boreal forest is expanding into the fragile tundra of the Northern Hemisphere, threatening a unique ecosystem which has been a vital food source for hundreds, perhaps thousands, of species, especially birds. When the boreal forest expands, it also causes other problems, notably fires and insect infestations, the ravages of which are accelerating.

These physical conditions have direct impacts on human beings. In 2002 the Worldwatch Institute reported that in the previous forty-two years the world economy had grown by seven trillion dollars every five to ten years, fueled by that soaring population just mentioned. The people of developed countries have benefitted disproportionately from the resulting prosperity, but the harmful consequences of such explosive growth are affecting everyone: increased threats from pollution, deforestation, and climate change, with accompanying losses of arable land, clean water, and biodiversity.

The essential lesson from these facts is that all the big issues and problems are related. The ecological health of the world where we live depends upon our behavior as humans. And that means all humans, regardless of national, racial, or religious affiliations. When we rely on gas-guzzling autos, we hasten the day when we will run out of irreplaceable fossil fuels. When we build yet another golf course, we further deprive the one billion human beings who lack even a gallon of clean water a day for drinking and preparing food. When multinational corporations dominate the trade in essential resources, developing countries cannot be self-sufficient, even in providing their own food. When we wage wars, or engage in acts of terror, or act as though our faith is the only valid one, we are destroying the willingness of people to cooperate. The big challenges facing us will not be resolved, cannot be resolved, until humans stop feuding with each other and realize that we are all a part of Nature, that saving the planet necessitates healing ourselves.

Absorbing the facts of global warming is not only painful, but pondering them drains my energy because I wish that they were not true. How much easier life would be without such bad news! But I discovered as a wayward teenager that ignoring my privileged but dysfunctional past was not helping me forge a more satisfying future. Nearly flunking out of high school was not going to get me into college. Feeling sorry for myself never did anything for me; happily, I never got a taste for it. Instead I had the good luck to realize that adversity might not be a deserved punishment from God, or even an inescapable fate delivered by the universe. It was just part of what was for dinner. If you don't like worms, try bugs. If you don't like bugs, try nuts. If you don't like nuts, get some claws and eat meat. Adapt.

Writing these essays has become a personal opportunity to shape up, to put my money where my mouth is, to walk the talk. And I've made a beginning. When I moved into my new home three and a half years ago, I installed a low-volume toilet. Next, I converted to compact fluorescent bulbs. I've stepped up my level of recycling. Recently, I conceived a program of xeriscaping a significant portion of my back yard. I rediscovered how much gasoline I could save by driving at the speed limit. (For years I've been driving a fuel-efficient Toyota Corolla.) I ask waitpersons in restaurants to save the water for a customer who requests it. I only use the dishwasher and laundry machines when they have full loads, and I find that my clothes get just as clean on the cold cycle as on the hot. I save a lot of energy by setting the water heater at the 120 degree mark, somewhat below what is average. When replacing appliances, I look for Energy Star brands.

During summer I have nearly eliminated a need for air conditioning by closing curtains during the day, then opening windows after the sun sets in the evening. My highest monthly energy bill over the last two summers has been $65. My house is just over 1,900 square feet. Meanwhile, I upgraded the insulation in my attic and walls. My highest energy bill the following winter was $110, and I was usually comfortable with the thermostat at 68 degrees, so long as I remembered to wear an undershirt, a warm shirt, and to pull on a sweater as needed. That's is a trick I learned in England, where people routinely keep their thermostats much lower than we do. Occasionally during winter, I have to push the thermostat up to 70, especially when writing, as my study is in the cooler basement. On the other hand, during summer that cooler space keeps me happy without turning on the air conditioning.

A friend reports that adding long underwear and heavy socks allows her to be comfortable at 65 degrees. She also suggests hanging out the wash to dry, instead of using the dryer. In winter, hanging it inside adds humidity, a desirable commodity in dry insulated houses. Cellular shades let in light but trap heat in winter, even when the day is exceptionally windy. Growing our own vegetables, even a few of them, saves money; if enough of us did it, the carbon costs of shipping them to groceries would decrease. And our health would improve.

Another imaginative friend has pledged to date only ladies who go topless, thereby saving the cost of shipping bra materials from China. Which makes me wonder, do the Chinese also manufacture jockey shorts for men? If so, let's have another Boxer Rebellion!

These are small steps, and I am only one person, but the longest journey begins with a single step, and the cumulative effect of millions of us doing similar small things can be enormous. Conservation is not only the cheapest, easiest, and most immediate remedy for the "energy crisis;" it is also by far the most effective.

9. You Can Run But You Cannot Hide

THE EVIDENCE FOR CLIMATE CHANGE is now massive and persuasive. Our own National Academy of Sciences has issued its own strong warning on the issue. Numerous major corporations have accepted it, and are acting to reduce their carbon footprint. So have many nations of the world, plus numerous regional and local governments. Policy makers now see it as a threat to national security. But skeptics persist. Significantly, most of them reside in the United States. Perhaps the best way to illustrate this is to mention attitudes. The results of a recent poll by the Pew Research Center (January 2009) showed that global warming was dead last among a list of twenty issues of concern to the public. "Environment" as an issue ranked only sixteenth. A Gallup Poll of 22 April 2010 revealed "historically low levels of public worry about environmental problems."

But the evidence of polls has always been ambiguous. Other polls suggest that most Americans seem to accept the reality of global warming and want to take action. It is difficult to gauge exactly how the public feels about the issue, however, because the results of opinion polls bounce up and down on all the relevant questions. And answers depend on how the questions are framed. But here's a more interesting question, with a lot less ambiguity, which reveals a lot more about attitudes. What would you say is the leading cause of global warming? If you said "human activity," only 41% of American voters agreed with you, according to a Rasmussen Reports poll of 27 January 2009, whereas 44% blamed "long-term planetary trends." Apparently, the other 15% don't know or don't care, itself an alarming fact. (Update: By February 2010 only 35% accepted human activity as the primary cause.)

What is notable in the poll just cited is a large disconnect between the American public and the scientists who study global warming. While two-thirds of the public does not accept human activity as the leading cause, scientists who study the problem overwhelmingly see human activity as the prime culprit, as is periodically confirmed by surveys published in leading scientific journals. In other words, the main cause of global warming has become a political issue.

How to explain this huge, and growing, disconnect between international scientists and most of the American public? It is a sad commentary on the shortsightedness of many of our business leaders that they focus more on next quarter's profit than on the looming disaster of global warming. There is no longer any rationale for ignoring our carbon emissions, and it is cynically dishonest to deliberately misinterpret scientific findings, yet that is precisely what lobbyists for Big Coal, conservative think tanks and their related vested interests are still doing. Surprised? Don't take my word for it: read Eric Pooley's *The Climate War* (2010). A professional business journalist, and former managing editor of *Fortune*, Pooley has interviewed the leaders on all sides of the controversy, and he demonstrates that many powerful business leaders still have their heads buried in the sand.

But thinking back to Pogo's "us," I have an explanation that goes deeper than the traditional blame game. Americans have been so fortunate for so long in their enjoyment of an increasingly convenient but wasteful lifestyle that they are unwilling to consider the costs of such profligacy. So habituated have we become to easy and continuous material growth that we now assume such prosperity is our birthright, and that anyone who mentions facts inconsistent with this mythology must be an ecoterrorist or a hateful socialist. Blaming stereotypical demons will not move us forward one inch in the struggle to contain global warming. But until we expose the nonsense behind the claims of those who deny the problem, we also won't get moving. So let's take a critical look at some of the notions that stand in the way of tackling the problem.

Some people still claim that the problems outlined in the last chapter (and others not mentioned) do not derive specifically from global warming, or more broadly from climate change. If you considered only one such problem at a time, you might find plausible explanations for some of them besides global warming. But these events do not exist independently. It is the combined effect of all of them which makes the case for global warming so compelling. No other explanation has been proposed that makes any sense of the extensive and overlapping observations.

Others believe that global warming is a fantasy of antibusiness elitists. But if global warming depended only on a political slant, it would have been exposed by scientists with better evidence. That hasn't happened. The reverse has happened: opponents of global warming deny scientific evidence, and instead concoct a series of misleading statements: for example, that CO_2 can't be dangerous, because it amounts to only 390 parts per million of the atmosphere. What they don't admit is how efficiently CO_2 absorbs and holds heat, even at tiny levels and especially in combination with other greenhouse gases. And those levels may not be as tiny as we used to think. A Swedish scientist, Dr. Bert Bolin, thinks the increased amount of CO_2 in Earth's atmosphere over the last century may have been as high as 8%, not the traditionally accepted 2%.

Another artful dodge is that CO_2 is absorbed naturally by the sea, the earth, and trees. It is, but our emissions are now increasing faster than they can be absorbed. Others argue that even if temperatures are rising, no catastrophes will result—a dangerous claim that is based on faith alone and ignores the cumulative evidence.

Other opponents assert that the scientific grounds for global warming are inconclusive, and, besides, are not even accepted by all scientists. Sound familiar? Cigarette companies said the connection of smoking with lung and respiratory disease was unproven. With similar motivation, anti-regulatory groups now "manufacture" doubt about the extent of human contributions to global warming. As long as the public remains mostly unaware of such sophistries, undertaking practical solutions to climate change will be delayed.

The assertion that not all scientists accept global warming is a deceptive fiction. Holding a Ph. D. in physics or chemistry, for example, does not a climate scientist make; often such "scientists" are shills for an industry whose costs would increase if it had to reduce emissions. Worse, ardent know-nothings with no credentials post their ingenious views on the Internet, hoping to blow away the problem with wishful thinking or greenwash. Awkwardly, the evidence opposes them.

The most revealing argument of opponents is that cutting back on emissions will harm the developed countries while giving the developing ones a free pass. This thinking ignores the possibilities of creating a new industrial revolution through green technology, then selling that technology to developing countries. This thinking dismisses conservation and the efficient creation of energy. This thinking remains silent about an economic system in which rich nations control the economic fate of poor ones. This thinking is stuck in the rut of wasteful consumerism, insisting on business as usual—in the same way Detroit ignored small cars until foreign automakers created a market for them. Can you hear King Canute, shouting at the tides to retreat?

Not surprisingly, those who deny any human responsibility for global warming have managed to make the issue a political one, in defiance of the scientific evidence. That same Rasmussen Report mentioned above found that 59% of Democrats blame global warming on human activity, but only 21% of Republicans agree. Sixty-seven percent of Republicans opt for long-term planetary trends, as opposed to only 23% of Democrats.

It is revealing that as recently as July of 2006 46% of all American voters thought human activities were the primary cause of global warming; only 35% identified long-term planetary trends. Apparently, with the Obama administration now in power, and determined to address global warming, those who don't want to acknowledge their contribution to the problem are stepping up their campaigns of misinformation.

Regarding the arguments about long-term trends of the planet, these refer to three cycles, called the Milankovitch cycles. These cycles describe the way Earth moves through the solar system, and the periodic changes in radiation Earth receives as a result. The cycles are valid and have been operating for eons, but the changes they engender unfold over tens of thousands of years, and none of them can explain the dramatic recent changes associated with climate change. Furthermore, the cycles cannot account for the dramatic recent rise in Earth's temperature, or the steady increase in greenhouse gases. Greenhouse gases are higher now than they have been for 650,000 years, possibly for 20 million years. Significantly, they began a steady rise with the Industrial Revolution, in the mid-eighteenth century, and they have been climbing ever since, ever more steeply. Nor is there any historical evidence that any particular congruence of the Milankovitch cycles has ever produced anything like our current situation in the past. In short, long-term planetary trends have nothing to do with the imminent crisis that faces us.

It is bad enough that climate change deniers are keeping the American public in a state of ignorance about the most challenging issue of the twenty-first century, largely to avoid the costs of changing their dangerous and inefficient ways. Such indifference is jeopardizing national security. An article in the *Christian Science Monitor* of 2 March 2010 ("War Over the Arctic? Global Warming Skeptics Distract Us from Security Risks") pointed out how all other Arctic nations except the United States are preparing to exploit the huge reserves of oil, natural gas, and valuable minerals—increasingly available as the ice sheets melt. Those other nations are also ramping up their military presence in the Arctic, to protect their natural assets.

Environmental awareness began in North America during the 1970s, focused on regional issues like water, air pollution, and acid rain. By the 1980s most of the world was aware, and the issues had become global. The Intergovernmental Panel on Climate Change (IPCC) was established in 1988 by the United Nations Environmental Program and the World Meteorological Organization. Based on the work of thousands of scientists from 130 countries, the IPCC periodically issues reports. The latest one, in February 2007, found the evidence for global warming "unequivocal," and the driving force behind it was "very likely" human activity, meaning greater than 90% probability.

These reports, in turn, have encouraged several international meetings in Rio de Janeiro (1992), Kyoto (1997), Bali (2007), Poznan (2008), Copenhagen (2009), and forthcoming in Cancun (Dec. 2010) where reformers have attempted (or will attempt again) to create binding agreements to reduce global warming. Ironically, as other nations took up what Americans had initiated, beginning in 1980 the United States adopted reactionary positions, either denying the problem or refusing to cooperate in meaningful ways to find solutions. It remains to be seen how effective the Obama administration will be in countering this embarrassing trend. Meanwhile every other major nation, including recent holdouts China and Australia, have recognized the problem and have pledged to work cooperatively in dealing with it, even though the specifics have yet to be worked out. As of 2008, even the developing nations have realized that they must take part in reducing carbon emissions.

But resistance to international cooperation is not simply a knee-jerk reaction of American conservatives. Isolationism in the United States has a long history, beginning with such stalwarts as George Washington and James Madison. It flourished because of the once-persuasive notion that if we remained aloof from the nationalistic rivalries of Europe, we could avoid the wars and other consequences of those rivalries. Such quaint notions have been overwhelmed since the end of World War II by the greater interconnectedness of nations, which renders our most serious problems global, not national. Environmental issues now frame the spearhead of internationalism, penetrating and gradually destroying older conceits of American exceptionalism. The question is, will America rejoin the international community in time to make a difference in alleviating the interrelated problems that lead to climate change?

For people who want to make that difference, how can they proceed? All peoples from the more fortunate nations can consider how to slow runaway population growth by helping to create more equity in the distribution of wealth around the globe. Most of the world's biodiversity exists in the developing countries, concentrated in tropical regions. Those regions are also home to the poorest peoples on Earth, where population is densest, and where concern about climate change is lowest. Unless the richer nations help the poorer ones to become participating partners in the global economy, the poor will, out of necessity, gobble up that precious biodiversity and increase greenhouse gas emissions in the process.

The wealthier nations can also ramp up their own sluggish economies by linking resource development and energy policy to conservation and green technology. At the same time we can take a new slant on the "war on terror" by realizing the link between green technology and security.

Tom Friedman put it best in his latest book, *Hot, Flat, and Crowded* (2008), in which he describes a 2007 visit to Iraq, where he saw firsthand how dangerous it was for our troops to be shuttling diesel fuel around the country. Our troops depend on diesel fuel to run their air conditioners in the 120 degree heat because the electric grid of Iraq is unreliable. Insurgents delight in planting bombs along the routes they know our convoys have to travel. The same is now occurring in Afghanistan. But to locate, transport, and use this limited supply of fossil fuel has become hugely expensive, as much as $42 a gallon. A far more economic and safer approach, Friedman points out, would be to utilize more solar and wind power. He quotes an energy consultant to the Army, who has been pushing for use of alternative fuels in the battlefields: "Energy independence is not an economic issue . . . . It's not a resource issue. It's a national security issue. It's the right business for us to be in."

Americans have been blessed with vast resources, nearly limitless opportunities, and a great deal of practical energy. We have been further blessed that, compared to most countries of the world, neither repressive governments inside nor hostile neighbors outside have prevented us from pursuing our good fortune. We have enjoyed so much success that we sometimes regard it as preordained, and assume that our future well-being is assured. Of course, it is not. Problems besetting the natural world now present both the greatest challenges to our future well-being, and our greatest opportunities to get beyond business as usual and emerge a stronger, more secure, more connected nation. To take advantage of those opportunities, however, we must begin to act now. If time and tide wait for no man, neither will climate change.

10. The Other Side of the Mountain

F. V. HAYDEN WAS THE premier explorer of the American West in the years following the Civil War. So rapid was his progress across the plains, collecting fossils and natural history specimens, that the Sioux called him "the man who picks up stones running." They judged him to be insane and thus no threat to them and not worth killing. There is a hasty, unfinished quality to many of Hayden's personal reports, although the abundant volumes published by his government-funded survey collected some of the best scientific papers of the nineteenth century. Hayden was a born promoter, a fervid naturalist, and a brilliant recruiter of talent. Westerners adored him, Congress could not resist him, and neither could most women. But his enthusiasm and lowly social origins earned him the scorn of some prominent Ivy League colleagues. Clearly a man of ability. I had to know more.

The Hayden Survey of the Territories operated across the West between 1867-79; its purpose was to discover the geology, outline the natural history and resources, and produce maps. For eleven years I pursed Hayden through the archives and across various parts of the West. But I wanted an up-close-and-personal connection to him and his survey, and I realized that Allen Wilson's division of the Hayden Survey, which operated across the entire San Juan Range in southwestern Colorado during the summer of 1874 was perfect for that purpose. So between Saturday, June 12 and Thursday, October 28, 1982, I retraced the route of Wilson's party, which involved climbing over sixty summits, logging roughly 450 miles on foot, and ascending over thirty vertical miles. In following Wilson's party I intended to understand its work by repeating part of it. I also wanted to gain more insights into Dr. Hayden himself, by following in his tracks, to see scenery like he had seen, to experience the same immersion in wilderness, the same encounters with wildlife, the same fear of the unknown, of getting lost or injured, even killed, and, ultimately, the same satisfaction of successful achievement.

Within the first two weeks of my journey, however, I faced a crisis. In my preliminary planning, I had underestimated how long it would take to cross dense forests, without benefit of reliable trails. I rubbed up a good set of blisters. My stomach rebelled at my own camp cooking. Solitude for days at a time was much different than for a day or two: it stimulated every mood between boredom and raw fear. Though surrounded by marvelous scenery, too often I felt scared, inadequate, and out-of-sorts. It also hit me what a big bite I had bitten off. The romance of the beginning of the trip had worn away and ahead lay an incredible amount of work, tension, even danger—and hopefully some discoveries and adventures.

Reality forced me to abandon my overly ambitious plan to walk between each of the fifty-four topographic stations established by Wilson's party. Of course, I was disappointed not to be able to walk the whole route, but I consoled myself with the realization that Wilson's party rode most of the way on mules. The surprises that occurred did not discourage me or drive me from the field. I adjusted and continued. I enlisted the Red Mule (my Subaru, the equivalent of Wilson's pack mules) to carry me and my gear between locales, from which I could scale a number of stations from nearby campsites. I discovered I could avoid the dreaded forests by scrambling up gullies and walking along ridges to my destinations.

And already there had been the kind of fruitful encounters I had hoped for. One morning, while waking in my tent, the flute-like melodies of a hermit thrush serenaded me. Two days later as I walked up through an aspen grove, I stopped to listen to the lovely stuttering song of a ruby-crowned kinglet. Atop Cannibal Plateau, above Lake City, I found one of the few original cairns Wilson and his party had built 108 years before, a solid eight-footer that made an ideal target for the theodolite they used to locate points and measure angles between them.

I was hiking up the jeep road to Engineer Pass, some twenty miles west of Lake City, in the second week of my ambitious summer. I had been up since five, and it was just after nine in the morning when I saw a large bird roaring across the sky. It was bigger than a raven—only a raptor would be that large. From a distance it resembled a turkey vulture, but its flight pattern was different. Flying fast, not soaring, the bird seemed to have a destination in mind, and I had no time to pull the binocular out of my pack to identify it. In only a few moments the bird flapped over a hill and disappeared.

I paused to recall other birds. Earlier that morning I had stopped to enjoy views of horned larks, American pipits, and two brown-capped rosy-finches—an adult and a youngster. The parent played with the fledgling, alternatively ignoring then darting at the imp, who all the while kept chirping and flapping for attention and begging for food. How fortunate I was to have seen those rosy-finches, because many birders come to Colorado specifically to add these hard-to-find beauties to their life lists. Many go home disappointed, yet, spending as much time as I did that summer on the alpine tundra, I enjoyed several visits with rosy-finches, and with white-tailed ptarmigan, another inconspicuous denizen of the tundra.

After reaching Engineer Pass, I turned north, along an ascending ridge that coincided with the Hinsdale-Ouray county line. I kept an eye out for the raptor. It was a typically exhilarating yet frightening day in the San Juan Mountains. Wetterhorn and Uncompahgre Peaks rose as sheer snow-covered walls, abruptly puncturing the skyline to the northeast. To the west Mt. Sneffels, Teakettle Mountain, and Potosi Peak raised their jagged heads. To the southwest Mount Wilson and El Diente Peak appeared, as they had over a hundred years before to the surveyors I was following, as a single massive hulk. Across from them I saw for the first time that summer the distinctive pyramid of Wilson Peak. To the south I could pick out all the Needle Mountains and the Grenadiers, the most wildly and continuously spiked country imaginable. Farther away to the southeast, more summits loomed in the distance, all of which I would climb later that summer. To the far north rose the Elk Range, though it would have been too far away for practical surveying in the 1870s. The sheer height and sweeping extent of these surrounding ranges stunned me temporarily. Unable to pull my wits together, I simply gazed. Only after a long, awe-struck interval did I begin to identify features and plot locations, the way my predecessors had done.

Simultaneously, huge moisture-laden thunderheads were building over the Gunnison Valley. A blister on my little toe throbbed painfully. Two days of diarrhea left me dehydrated and apprehensive. After locating Station 10, north of Engineer Pass, I was supposed to head west toward Hayden Mountain, on the other side of the Uncompahgre River. No telling where I'd be able to cross that river, but between the ridge and the river stretched many miles, made difficult by smaller drainages, wide meadows, and fingers of forest, all of them booby trapped with unstable snow.

Trekking up the east side of the Pass, I had already been surprised and delayed by deep snowdrifts. I was lugging a fifty-one pound pack, which prevented rapid progress. Several feet of old, packed snow covered the road, and nearly a foot of fresh, wet snow made the going even slower. I frequently broke through the soft layers, and my legs created deep holes in the snow; this "postholing" quickly drained my energy. And I was alone, quite alone. Most of the time, solitude has soothed and nourished me, but at this moment I wanted someone with me to share the dramatic views, and to bolster my sinking spirits.

Right on cue, and interrupting the emotional storm brewing inside me, the big bird reappeared. It flew low over ground just beneath me, in pursuit of some creature, and I gladly dropped the pack in order to retrieve my binocular. Though he missed a meal, the bird perched on a rock and gave me several timeless moments to observe him. It was a golden eagle, a magnificent bird, but not one I expected to see at nearly 13,000 feet. Perhaps he found no prey lower down, or perhaps, like me, he enjoyed the thrill of heights. Delighted with my luck, but concerned for the fate of this bird, I suddenly realized how much his presence meant to me. Watching him, my chest contracted and tears poured down my face in a bittersweet mix of joy and sadness. Here in an isolated corner of Hinsdale County, amidst awesome scenery but also threatening weather and dangerous terrain, was a living symbol of wilderness. Even if he had roamed a bit out of habitat, the eagle belonged here. I was the fortunate visitor who just happened to meet him in his realm. It is from that moment, on the morning of the twenty-second of June 1982, that I date my initiation into the fraternity of nature advocates.

I have been a nature lover all my life, in the passive sense that I had always enjoyed the outdoor world, and I had been expressing and deepening that love by walking through varied landscapes, climbing numerous mountains, admiring diverse creatures, but especially by pursuing birds, who early on showed me the connectedness of all Nature's creatures, and who first inspired me to think of something larger and more enduring than myself. But after that encounter with the eagle I changed. In one of those revealing moments I realized that the eagle, though superbly adapted to wilderness, had problems of his own, problems that I and others of my species made larger. Henceforth I knew I had a responsibility to become an activist: to protect that eagle, and to begin speaking out about what we humans will miss if we allow eagles and wilderness to disappear, or even to lessen their hold on our psyches.

A month later, on July 26, I had other valuable insights. They came at the end of another day of solitude and surprises. I started the day in Lake City, after saying goodbye to my climbing buddy, Peter Dessauer, with whom I had just enjoyed five splendid days of climbing and exploration. Several friends joined me for extended weekends of that summer, or planned parts of their vacations to coincide with my venture. Now it was back into the wilderness on my own.

Driving southwest out of Lake City, just beyond Lake San Cristobal, and only a few yards off the dirt road, I spotted a bear cub. Only four feet tall standing on its hind legs, and wearing a cinnamon-colored coat of fur, it was probably a young black bear, but just possibly a young grizzly. Despite years of hiking in some pretty remote places, I had never seen a bear in the wild before. I spotted him from the road and jumped out of the car for photos. Momma bear was nowhere nearby—perhaps she was no longer alive, for junior seemed agitated and disoriented. He noticed me but bothered himself not a bit and went right on half playing tag with himself, half looking around and running off in one direction, then back in another.

Though thrilled at finding the bear, I reflected how glad I was to have my car, in case momma bear should appear, but I knew I would soon have to leave the safety of the car in order to experience again the isolation and unpredictability that swallow anyone in the wilderness. I continued on up the Lake Fork of the Gunnison River to the vicinity of Cottonwood Creek, intending to search for Station 13. It was an undistinguished summit of 12,720' in between two higher points, both over fourteen thousand feet (Wilson's Stations 12 and 14), that Peter and I had climbed the previous week.

From studying the map, I could not understand why my predecessors had bothered to climb this lesser point, but from its summit I relearned a useful lesson. From the top of Sunshine Peak (Station 12), Wilson's division intended to move west to Handies Peak (Station 14), a logical next station. From Sunshine it looks like you can walk toward Handies via what seems to be a connecting ridge, which appears to go through this lower Station 13. Alas, as Wilson's party discovered when attempting it, the ridge does not make an easy or direct connection; it leaves a steep descent before climbing back up to Handies. This was only a single dramatic illustration of what Wilson's party had to discover over and over: appearances can be deceiving. Even with the benefit of good maps (Wilson didn't have any worth the name), and modern roads (Wilson had no roads and few trails to guide him), I also had to relearn this lesson many times that summer. In the wilderness there are often no shortcuts, and the best route is often discovered only after trial and error.

Wilderness still harbors wild beasts, some quite ferocious, as I discovered while walking up the ridge to Station 13. Though the route was easy, it became intolerable because of hordes of aggressive flies that ignored my two applications of bug juice and persisted in making my life miserable all the way up. This race was clearly not as advanced as those on the nearby fourteeners, for they had not learned to wait until their victim was moving, and therefore more vulnerable to attack. Since this hump was obviously rarely visited by man (no reason really, except perhaps in hunting season), I was something of a curiosity and every villager was called out. Just as obviously, they were unprepared for the analytical and vengeful character of man, for I found I could kill them more readily by swatting or clapping. But they did learn fast, and as I progressed uphill, from one territory, or village, to another, it seemed the scouts went ahead to announce me to the next tribe and warn them that I had, whatever I was, a more potent swisher than the deer, elk, or mountain goats that browsed here. I reflected that flies are like jackals, sharks, or buzzards—making their living off someone else. Despicable lot. Lazy too. Bees are different. Numerous though they were, and despite my inadvertently striding through shrubs they were visiting, the bees were too busy to be distracted by my temporary presence, and too intelligent to make any fuss.

So much for my morning. The Red Mule delivered me near the base of my next destination, Station 53, along the Rio Grande River, just east of the large reservoir along that river that is west of the town of Creede and south of Spring Creek Pass. It provided a disappointing view, and the clouds opened their pores onto me all the way up. But I gained a satisfying feeling of comradeship with Hayden and his "boys." I wasn't doing all this just for the enjoyment of being in the mountains, with all that implied about adventure, beauty, self-discovery, or fanciful notions about merging with the wilderness. I had a job to do and wanted to get it done. I stood in the woods waiting for the rain to cease. As it stopped, I experienced an eerie interlude. All life seemed suspended, waiting to see if the storm would continue or whether movement and song could recommence. Romantics would have found wonders in these moments. So might I in another mood. At the time I noticed only the pervasive quiet and a sense of total emptiness. It reminded me of what some people think death leads to: restfulness, they say. Boring, I say. And frightening.

I had never felt that way about Nature before, and rarely since. But by the middle of that summer I had been drawn into a more intimate relationship with Mother Nature. Because of my prolonged exposure, I had penetrated beyond the romance and wonder I had always found before and seen a side of her that was awesome but strange, even alien. Despite her frequent beauty, Nature's moods will often discourage humans from cozying up to her. I had known that before, but now from my wilderness-saturated perspective, I understood in a new way the attitude that wants to tame Nature, exploit her, see her as an other, separate from ourselves: out of fear, we want to protect ourselves from Nature's strangeness. It requires an act of will to escape the primitive instinct to strike back and to realize the best reason for protecting and preserving Nature is that she is so different, so robustly diverse.

Prolonged exposure to Nature that summer also provoked a number of thoughts on the relationship of solitude and companionship. While driving between stations on that July 26th, I got to thinking about being alone so much. Sure, I had learned to do it very well, and at times I need it. But as a general and permanent state I don't like it. I missed not having a companion today: the pictures I took in towns, and the setting would have been more fun to share with someone. I don't get lonesome as often in the mountains, especially when I'm working up some peak, though with the right person even that would be more enjoyable.

I recalled a tender moment that had occurred a couple of weeks before with Elaine, the lady I was dating at the time. She had joined me for a weekend of hiking and exploring, and on the way down from a summit I remember saying to her, "This is the way I'd like to spend every day." The larger implications of my words (mutually grasped by both of us) included not just an outdoor adventure with a pleasant companion, but, at the end of the day, looking forward to a shower, something more appealing than a cold supper or a warmed up freeze-dried one, and a warm, dry bed.

Also implied but not uttered aloud were the words: "How wonderful it would be if you could join me every night in that bed!" Thinking about Elaine that summer stirred up the usual quandaries single people confront. I wondered what I really wanted in a relationship, who Elaine really was and what she might want, and what commitments either of us might be willing to make. In the event, she and I did not take that next committing step. We remained a temporary attachment, never became a permanent connection. At the time I felt sad about that, and I think she did too. Years later with a couple more unsuccessful marriages behind me, I had learned to see nothing wrong with temporary attachments. Not every relationship should endure, or flower into a permanent connection. People can remain friends, as Elaine and I have, even if they go their separate ways. The tension between solitude and togetherness is never completely resolved, even for "happily married couples," whoever they might be.

A *New Yorker* cartoon (author Barbara Smaller, 7 September 2009) speaks perfectly to this point. A couple is saying goodnight after an obviously close and confiding discussion, which ends with the woman saying to the man, "I, too, want companionship, intimacy, and someone to grow old with, but not 24/7."

Collections of people can be anything from a clique to a crowd. Most have no more permanence than a passing cloud, and no more impact than a spring rain. They only become couples or communities when their members recognize, respect, and nourish each other as such. A committed relationship, like a community, implies mutually accepted goals and values. If couples or communities have those, then their togetherness becomes something that can grow and evolve. But losing their mutuality, or the desire to stay together as permanent connections, couples fall apart and communities disintegrate.

It is no different in the wider realm of Nature. Nature's community already exits, and, whether we accept it or not, that community includes us. It was not always so, for Nature existed for eons without us, but, having evolved, or having been created if you prefer, we are now an inseparable part of Nature. If Nature is to flourish, if we are to prosper as a species, humans must recognize their intricate ties to the natural world and behave responsibly toward it and among ourselves. Numerous individuals must choose Nature as a permanent connection, not just a temporary attachment. How many individuals will be required? That is the Sixty-Four Dollar Question. The answer will be decided by an ongoing experiment involving all of us. In a real sense, we are Nature's experiment, and if we do not willingly embrace her, she may choose to dispose of us at her leisure.

11. South Table Mountain: Spring

WHILE WINTER IS AN ATHENAEUM, a solemn temple where scholars come to reflect upon our infinite connections with the unity and diversity of life, spring is a runaway express train, hurtling across the landscape at full throttle, whistle blowing, technicolor lights blasting from every portal. I can't get aboard this rocket. I can barely get out of the way to avoid being crushed. So much mating to do. So many chicks to raise. So many predators to avoid. And I am not the only creature threatened by the galloping urgency of spring. Insects scamper madly, often right into the beaks of birds. Song birds constantly broadcast their locations, a dangerous ritual that only aids the stealthy advance of foxes, the snapping jaws of coyotes, and the swooping scythes of raptors.

Spring is not so much a season as an explosion. It doesn't happen. It erupts. It overwhelms me and fills me with such primal feelings that I lose any sense of myself as a separate being capable of interpreting another. I become that other being, and all the rest too.

Consider some of the music that has been composed in honor of spring. I think first of Vivaldi, whose perceptive ode to the *Four Seasons* expresses the bouncy joy of being alive. Stravinsky's *The Rite of Spring* celebrates the scrambled intensity of the season. Beethoven's Sixth Symphony, the *Pastorale*, embraces melody and mirth, both suitable for spring, and the last movement especially feels a lot like spring. But none of these composers, who deliberately conjured the spirit of spring, quite captures the necessary seismic upheaval, at least not for me.

Another composer does capture it, a man who may never have thought about spring in connection with his music: Wilhelm Richard Wagner. Not surprisingly, Wagner was inspired by Beethoven, and in his love of theatre, his dramatic approach to music and life, his fascination with mythology, his embracing of radical social ideas (even the dark and now embarrassing ones) Wagner, in all of his music, but I suppose supremely in *The Ring of the Nibelung* cycle, expresses the truth of spring. It is an upwelling from the depths. It sucks its energy from the earth, and all the mysterious elements that intermingle there, then surges upward in sprouts and sprigs and shoots, trunks and stems and branches, forcefully shoving aside last year's growth to make way for newer forms of life. And I respond to spring in the same way, from the depths. From my genes. From the deeply programmed urge to recreate.

Yet we deceive ourselves if we completely accept this explosive interpretation of spring. The deception, which all of us practice, occurs subconsciously. We slog our way through winter, bundled against the elements and wary of the expanding darkness. We whine about the cold, the wind, the accumulating drifts, or the oozing slush, until one day we notice trees in bloom, birds singing, the air balmy. We knew spring would come, but its sudden arrival always surprises. Therein lies the deception. During winter, with our heads down, our eyes cast inward, and our endorphins at a low level, we fail to notice the incremental changes that take place every day. By missing these cumulative clues we experience spring as a single glorious explosion, rather than a gradual shifting of ambiguous signals, so gradual as to defy the definition of separate seasons. How many buds must burst, how many birds must sing, how many signals must we notice before declaring spring? Perhaps these questions suit philosophy more than science. But I want to give science a chance anyway. Here are selections from my field notes during a recent transitional season at STM. You decide when spring begins.

Mar. 8: 3.5 hrs. Temp. 34-36 F. 17 species, including mountain bluebird, the first bird to return from Arizona/New Mexico, but all winter residents still here. Baffled by fog, bluebird perched in same tree for over 2 hrs; I explored grassland, then returned to find him still there.

Mar. 18: 4 hrs. Temp. 22-38 F. 22 species (9 around houses). New arrivals: mountain bluebird (now 3 of them), song sparrow, western meadowlark. But mostly still winter residents, esp. juncos, rough-legged hawk, Townsend's solitaire.

Mar. 30: 34-44 F. 3.5 hrs. 21 species but no new spring birds. Bluebirds have moved on to higher pastures.

Apr. 8: 38-46 F. 3.5 hrs. 17 species. New arrivals: rock wren, sage thrasher, common grackle.

Apr. 17: 3.5 hrs. 42-45 F. 23 species. More new arrivals: common raven, barn swallow, chipping sparrow. And a downy woodpecker, not seen since December.

Apr. 29: 3 hrs. 44-63 F. 22 species. Recently arrived: Swainson's hawk, violet-green swallow, house wren, yellow-rumped warbler, vesper sparrow, white-crowned sparrow, brown-headed cowbird. Plus two year-rounders not seen since early winter: canyon wren, and great-horned owl.

May 13: 45-55 F. 4.25 hrs. 29 species. More new arrivals: white-throated swift, Lewis's woodpecker, western wood-pewee, western kingbird, blue-gray gnatcatcher, Virginia's warbler, western tanager, lark sparrow, Bullock's oriole.

We seem to have dissenting opinions regarding the onset of spring! It depends on which species you ask. But the deception becomes clear by early May. Some time around that date my five senses become choked with the evidence. I inhale the scent of flowers and become tipsy with their aromas. I witness frantic flights to and fro, hither and yon. I taste urgency in the air, as I feel warm zephyrs brush my face. Above all, I hear the dueling males of several species, warning away rivals as they plead for sex.

While winter is a formal dinner party, held in a cool ballroom, where polite guests honor celebrities, spring is a raucous outdoor picnic, a charivari sponsored by the gods of misrule, where children stage food fights, defy all decorum, and periodically escape the apron strings of their parents, some never to return. I love this uninhibited spectacle. At no other time of the year can I observe, at such close proximity, the intimate lifestyle of birds. Yet I am never more distant. Birding is always a selfish, intrusive occupation, never more so than during spring, when birds are the most vulnerable. Just being present, I interrupt, interfere, intimidate. I don't mean to do so, but to approach these exotic flying dragons, to admire their beauty, to learn of their fascinating ways, inevitably I disturb them. I have learned to love them, not as I would a lover, but as an esteemed friend, with whom a little distance is appropriate.

So I back off from the dense shrubs just below the south slope of the mesa, the scene of so much frenetic activity, and stroll up to the grasslands. A vesper sparrow greets me on top (he's actually warning his colleagues of an intruder), his voice so reminiscent of the song sparrow but identifiable because of the very different habitat. Song sparrows prefer riparian corridors crowded with trees. Vespers like dry gullies and open spaces. As long as they can find a clump of shrub to cling to, they are happy. A western Meadowlark trumpets my arrival. His song— so sharp, so clear, so penetrating—carries a long distance, across the sweeping prairie. Unlike the delicate trills of the vesper sparrow, this clarion call obscures its sender; it seems to blare from high fidelity speakers all around me. So powerful is the voice that I frequently underestimate the distance from which it emanates. I finally find him, sitting atop a mullein stalk, probably 150 yards away. He sounds much closer.

I walk westward, along the south rim. I'll go north along the west rim as far as Castle Rock, then turn east and head back to my starting point, a parking lot near the National Renewable Energy Lab at the foot of the southern slope. Along the way I'll traverse or observe four of the habitats of STM: short-grass prairie, foothills shrub, a patch of what resembles semi-desert shrub, and urban areas at the base of the mesa. At other times I'll make a point of intersecting the other four habitats: lowland riparian (along a canal beneath the north slope), foothills riparian (originating from a spring in the north central portion), mountain grassland (interspersed with the prairie grasses), and the cliffs that surround the mesa and give it its distinctive form. Because STM shares characteristics of both the plains and foothills life zones, its eight habitats have a mixed quality that reflect the structure of the local plant and bird communities, as well as the elevation, slope, and aspect of the local geography.

In order to sample its diversity and overlapping habitats, I have divided the mesa into twenty-nine different routes, each of which I try to walk regularly in spring. Given the extent of the place, I normally do only three or four routes in half a day. The routes select groupings of pure grass, pure shrubs, urban suburbs, and cliffs, then mixtures of those, for example, shrub-suburbs, shrub-grasses, and shrub-riparian. Today is the twenty-first of May, and all doubt about the season has vanished. Spring reigns in all its raging, mindless glory, driven by instinct and habit. Rather than the detached observer of winter, I too, like all the birds, mammals, insects, and rodents hereabouts, have become a focused hunter. My only weapon is a 10 by 42 binocular, and my purpose is not to destroy but to discover life.

But make no mistake. Walking across the grasslands, I am a hunter. I would find few birds If I did not spot likely roosts or nests hundreds of yards away, then sneak up to them. The grassland offers few places to hide, and be they ever so preoccupied with breeding, birds can see me coming from a long way off. So I approach in roundabout fashion. I stop often to look and listen. I never hurry, and I encourage my prey to become comfortable with my deliberate but casual advance.

But the rewards of this patient stalking are immense. Every fifty yards or so, a different towhee sings for a mate, as does a different meadowlark. Chipping sparrows skim across the terrain in noisy gangs. Another emberizine is Brewer's sparrow, and a less colorful, less distinctive bird you would be hard pressed to name. Its blandness, when added to its cryptic habits, make this bird very difficult to find. Best to listen for its buzzy trill, but, unlike most of his cousins, *Spizella breweri* is very shy and will likely not sing if you are nearby. I must estimate his probable nesting site, then sit tight for what could be a long wait while the bird relaxes enough to sing. Such is the reward of the hunter.

Spotting the handsome sage thrasher brings a more dramatic recompense, and one that requires no waiting. Like most birds in a grassland habitat, this mimic with a clear warbling voice disguises himself in drab plumage, but he likes to sit in the top branches of a tall, isolated shrub. His front is streaked attractively, and seeing his bold yellow iris reminds me of the first time I got kissed, really kissed, by someone I truly fancied. Whamo!

Another mimic, and another bird capable of sending chills of delight through my nervous system, is the yellow-breasted chat. I meet him while descending from the grasslands, in thick shrub where he can warble and croak and whistle in disarming fashion while I look in vain for him. Like other shrub-dwelling ventriloquists, he has me looking everywhere but where he sits. Despite his bright yellow color, his moderate size, and his willingness to perch in the open, many times I have had to content myself with listening to his unorthodox repertoire. Such are the tactics of the hunted.

The gray catbird is equally difficult to locate, just from the sound of his voice, but, possessed of a curious temperament, he will bounce around in the shrubbery and sooner or later reveal himself, ever so briefly. The blue-gray gnatcatcher employs a different strategy. Despite his tiny size, this lion of a bird learned somewhere along the path of evolution that he could scare away gigantic foes with aggressive behavior and a raspy voice.

Soaring over the cliffs above me like supersonic fighter jets are white-throated swifts. With swept-back wings they hurl through the air at great speed with no apparent effort, catching insects on the wing, but clearly enjoying the pleasure of zooming every bit as much as hunting. At lower ledges of the rocks, cliff swallows swarm back and forth in a hypnotic pattern, their flight, their colonial behavior, and their gentle squawking reminding me of bats. I walk closer to the base of the cliffs, in hopes of rousing one of my favorite birds, the rock wren. Like the gnatcatcher, this wren believes that the best defense is a good offense. Perched on a conspicuous ledge, he throws sound at me, yet his trill is playful, hardly threatening. What gets my attention is the rump-pump action accompanying his song. Hilarious to me, but probably frightening to a smaller intruder. He seems to be signaling, "Come another step closer and I'll poop on you!"

It's always fun to save the best for last. Not that I can plan such good fortune, but today it happens. Descending a gulch toward my car I spy a familiar but surprising shape in a cottonwood. A look through the glasses confirms: an ash-throated flycatcher! A genuine treat, because I expect to see this guy in the dry canyon lands in the western part of the state. Crested, with a white chest and a pale yellow belly, and sporting a long tail with a reddish tinge, this flycatcher has an unmistakable call, which he disdains to give me. He is traveling to his summer breeding grounds. He is not accompanied by a female, so why waste any breath on me? There is a calmness about this bird, which is refreshing after the pell-mell dashing I have been witnessing all morning and which has reduced me to a giddy state somewhere between exhilaration and exhaustion. It's been worth every minute: thirty-one species in three and a half hours; a total of 175 birds. Now I'm going to need a nap.

12. Voodoo Economics, Adam Smith, and Corporate Capitalism

You've heard of Ponzi schemes, and pyramid ploys, and chain letters that will bring you vast wealth. Whether practiced anonymously on millions, through a stock market swindle or an e-mail scam, or visited privately on a gulled investor, all these cons depend upon sleight-of-hand from the perpetrator and avarice from the victim. Supply-side economics is such a scheme, but this one is brought to us courtesy of that sick but sacred cow we dignify with the name of American free market capitalism, and it has been sanctioned by the federal government.

Since 1980, when Ronald Reagan was elected President of these United States, and until the financial disasters of 2008-09, ideas called supply-side economics enjoyed heady circulation and the endorsement of every free-marketer, deregulator, and tax cutter in the land. Supply-side notions suggest that if you cut taxes, especially among the richest Americans, who have the greatest potential for investment, economic productivity and expansion would follow. Government revenues would increase because of a swelling tide of prosperity. Even the poor and middle classes would benefit because of the "trickle down effects" of the miraculous supply-side manna from heaven.

Milton Friedman (1912-2006) became the high priest of this cult, and he recruited a number of true believers who wanted to decrease the size of government by starving it of revenue. It is important to connect the dots

71

here. Notice how well the supply-side ideology suits those who deny global warming, because effectively confronting global warming would mean greater regulation of the economy—an abomination every supply-sider would condemn.

Supply-side ideas were suspect from the start. Former President George Herbert Walker Bush called them "voodoo economics" while contesting Reagan for the Republican nomination. Recently, Paul Krugman, a Nobel laureate in economics and a professor at Princeton, has called them "snake oil economics." Studies by the Congressional Budget Office confirm that Reagan's tax cuts in the 1980s, like those of George W. Bush in 2003, did not increase government revenues. Instead they ballooned the federal deficit, and increased the disparity between incomes. In 2003 both the nonpartisan Economic Policy Institute and the conservative Wall Street Journal opposed tax cuts. Tax cuts failed to raise general prosperity. Worse, supply-side rhetoric stoked financing of the dot-com bubble, which burst in 2001, and the sub-prime mortgage bubble, which burst in 2008, both of which leveraged huge amounts of debt into speculative investment. You know the result: the 2008-09 recession, massive job losses, general misery. How much did you lose? But the free market boosters who sold us on supply-side snake oil profited mightily. And as of June 2010, our Congress was still piously debating inadequate reforms.

Just as supply-side ideologues have ignored the grim results of implementing their ideas uncritically, so in worshiping Adam Smith as their patron saint they have distorted Smith's broader meaning. Back in 1776 Adam Smith published *The Wealth of Nations*. The book soon became a classic and subsequently the ideal model for conservative economists, which is odd, because in his day readers hailed Smith as a very liberal thinker. Of course, both the words "liberal" and "conservative" have undergone such considerable and strange evolutions since the eighteenth century that their original meanings are scarcely recognizable today.

Be that as it may, you can understand why *The Wealth of Nations* would appeal to the supply-side folk. Smith argued that wealth and human progress would grow in step with each other if individuals, in their roles as buyers and sellers of goods, were permitted maximum personal freedom. Quaintly, he foresaw no complications: just get government out of the way and individuals acting in their own self-interest would find the best methods of creating prosperity, guided "as if by an invisible hand." Lest that quote sound like a subtle plug for the deity, I should clarify Smith's take on religion, for he rather scorned the established Anglican church. Instead, he favored "natural theology," which assumed the use of reason, as opposed to revelation, in gaining knowledge of the natural world. Well, amen to that.

To put Smith in historical context, he lived and wrote during the infancy of the Industrial Revolution. Land was still the chief form of capital, and agriculture the main generator of wealth. Smith felt that only labor which produced a commodity was productive, thus he did not anticipate how much machinery—working without actual laborers— would soon drive manufacturing, nor did he foresee the huge potential of what we call the service economy. In Smith's lifetime (1723-90) economic processes were not as complicated nor as technologically based as they would later become. But Smith was dead right in pointing out that the full benefits of manufacture could only be realized if states opened their markets to free trade, expanded the use of credit and paper money, and moved away from the restrictive doctrines of mercantilism that had guided the thinking of statesmen since the sixteenth century.

Mercantilism pushed for a favorable balance of trade (selling more goods abroad than you bought as imports), which meant that governments intervened mightily in the economy to regulate industry, agriculture, and trade. Governments also subsidized industries, and protected them from foreign competitors with tariffs. As a result, the state gathered handsome revenues, but individual buyers and sellers plodded along. Entrepreneurs barely got out of the starting gate. Thus Smith, the hero of a liberated economy.

To give the devil his due, Smith ushered in an age of free trade and greatly expanded the horizons, and ambitions, of capitalists. Unhappily, free trade barely outlived the idealistic Age of Enlightenment which had hatched it. Increasingly nationalistic states of the nineteenth century, with an eye to protecting their colonies, returned to a neo-mercantilism that stressed self-sufficiency and extensive controls instead of specialization of production and the maximum circulation of goods.

But there is a great deal more to Adam Smith than those who tout him care to admit. To Smith the standard of all economic value was labor. He said: "Equal quantities of labour at all times and places are of equal value to the labourer," which meant that the amount of labor required for their production was the only useful way to compare the value of commodities. That view does not sit well with supply-side thinkers, many of whom want to abolish labor unions, and who, at the end of 2008, approved a massive bailout for financial and credit institutions, but resisted a much more modest assistance to the American auto industry, the main purpose of which was to stave off massive unemployment.

Smith also urged governments to spend money on things we would call infrastructure, on the grounds that individuals would not recover their expenses or make any profit from such investments. Had the word "infrastructure" been used in Smith's day, he would have included education in it, because he felt education was a prime example of the sort of expenditure that government should pay for. He intended education to include basic literacy and arithmetic, sufficient to carry on any trade or occupation, and to exercise the duties of citizenship. Which sounds like he favored free universal education through the secondary level.

Infrastructure means the basic facilities supporting a country, and, as Smith understood, public funds should sustain these benefits, instead of relying on the self-interest of individuals or the erratic behavior of markets. It is interesting that all modern developed states, except the United States, include the following in infrastructure: utilities, communications, and energy, as well as such services as noncommercial radio and television, generous grants for education and the arts, and national health programs. Unlike today's supply-side thinkers, Adam Smith understood that economics works most effectively as a mixed system: that is, with free enterprise and the market supplying most private wealth, and government providing those goods and services to all citizens, including the wealthy, that are necessary to protect and promote the public good.

While conservatives have done Adam Smith a great disservice by distorting his meaning, it was never their intention to portray him accurately or discuss him fully. Supply-siders venerate and promote Adam Smith mainly because he exalted unfettered individualism, and they see modern corporate capitalism as the fulfillment of Smith's vision for that individualism. Smith assumed that wealth and human progress amounted to pretty much the same thing, thus endorsing a materialistic view of the human condition. Economists, and nearly all Americans until the late twentieth century, made the same assumption. But recently we have discovered many ways that exploiting resources can degrade our physical surroundings and harm our health. So Mr. Smith has done Nature, and all of us who depend on its healthy condition, no favors, but of course Smith could not have foreseen the results of linking his ideas to modern corporate capitalism.

Exalting unbridled individualism was Smith's most baleful influence, but again the context matters. Like virtually all his colleagues in the Enlightenment, Smith wanted to release the creative powers of individuals by lifting the heavy hand of authority, both secular and religious. He did not foresee that newly enriched entrepreneurs might become parasites, or that corporations would wield as cruel and tyrannical an authority as ever any state has exercised. Humans may not be inherently parasitic, but that's what we become when we renounce conscience. Protected against unlimited liability, and with legal responsibility only to shareholders, corporations can renounce both conscience and loyalty—loyalty to any assortment of people, to any city or state, to any nation or region, or to any entity except itself. Sufficient unto itself is corporate capitalism, and indifferent to the wider problems of society, even those it creates.

And while Smith certainly did not invent the concept of Progress, he and his pals in the Enlightenment gave it a huge boost. They persuaded mankind henceforth to expect ever-better days in the future. Before the eighteenth century people did not assume progress, or habitually equate the future with improvement. To the contrary, the moral and intellectual compass of thinkers before the Enlightenment pointed backwards in time, to the golden age of classical Greece and Rome. In wanting to distance themselves from the prejudices of the *ancien régime*, eighteenth-century reformers threw out the baby with the bath water, by assuming that because they had gained knowledge unknown to the classical giants, they had also surpassed them in wisdom. Wrong! The wisdom of the classical world consisted in its deep understanding of human nature. Its philosophers, scientists, and dramatists knew that humans could improve the conditions of their lives, but they were skeptical about improving human nature itself.

It is by now a tragic irony that corporate capitalism, though the most efficient engine of creating wealth, has become the greatest threat to genuine human progress—meaning better health, improved education, wider opportunity, economic and social justice, a more generous appreciation of our cultural differences, and a greater awareness of our common ties to the natural world.

By preaching its mission of constant growth, the proponents of modern corporate capitalism have crafted the greatest utopia ever imagined. Unlimited growth is not only a logical absurdity, it defies the reality of limited resources. It is, if you will, the ultimate speculative bubble, and if allowed to continue unchecked will burst like all the rest. But this need not be humanity's fate. In most fields of human endeavor we have moved a huge distance down that admittedly winding and bumpy road toward what I just defined (at the end of the previous paragraph) as genuine human progress. It is our worship of the false gods of greed and growth that impede us.

It was not always so. For all of human existence until the eighteenth century, and embracing diverse cultures and civilizations, mankind's primary economic preoccupation has been sufficiency, not growth. Sufficiency asks how much, not how much more. Sufficiency considers priorities, not just profits; it distinguishes real needs from trinkets; it aims for our overall welfare and happiness, not just our passing pleasures or corrupting comforts. Sufficiency does not condemn us to a bleak landscape of mere subsistence, as its critics would have you believe. Instead, it pursues our material survival in the more cheerful context of human potential. We must lift our heads out of the troughs and look beyond the feedlots where we live in order to remember who we truly are, and what we might become again.

13. Let There Be CFLs

WHAT CAN ONE PERSON DO that would make any difference for the planet? Installing compact fluorescent light bulbs (CFLs) is one answer. The reasons to do so are compelling: save money, conserve energy, reduce carbon emissions. According to *Consumer Reports*, "Despite having less than 5% of the world's population, the United States is responsible for almost a quarter of global carbon emissions." As I screwed in my first CFL two years ago, I felt good, as if I were playing on a new kind of team. I thought about another quote from *Consumer Reports*: "If every household [in the U. S.] replaced just one bulb, the energy savings could light more than 3 million households for a year."

CFLs save you money. Despite a higher initial cost, CFLs last up to ten times longer than incandescent bulbs, and they use less energy while they work. How long they last depends on the wattage, the type, and on how much you use them. Generally, replace those bulbs first that will be "on" the most. You will even save energy with those you turn on only briefly, but you will use up the bulb faster.

A traditional 100 watt incandescent bulb uses 100 watts of energy, but the equivalent CFL produces the same light using only 26 watts of energy. It takes about 80 pounds of coal to power one incandescent bulb over its lifetime; to power the equivalent CFL requires less than a pound of coal. "Lighting accounts for a third of U. S. electricity use, more than half of which is generated by coal—the primary source of our carbon dioxide emissions." CFLs have caught up with the times. They no longer hum or flicker. They come in a variety of styles, sizes, and shapes. There are even dimmers, flood lamps, and 3-stage bulbs.

CFLs gained mass market status because the Energy Department asked manufacturers in 1998 to produce an affordable CFL. They used to cost as much as $30 apiece. The government provided money to reduce costs, and helped producers find mass market buyers, like Wal-Mart, Costco, and Home Depot.

Consumers have reported some problems. CFLs installed in enclosed ceiling fixtures, for example, generate more heat, which can burn the bulb out faster. There have been quality problems because some manufacturers have cut corners, resulting in bulbs that don't work or that burn out before they should. The government has pledged to increase inspections as a result. Should you refrain from buying CFLs because there are still bugs to be worked out? Of course not. Would you abandon your computer because weirdness in cyberspace continues to exasperate virtually all of us with unexpected crashes, files that disappear, or viruses that may invade?

CFLs may not appear to be as bright as traditional bulbs. I found it depends on the circumstances. I used to have two 100 watt incandescent bulbs in the laundry room, which I replaced with two 26 watt CFLs. Though the room seemed less bright, it was plenty bright enough for my purposes. But the situation was reversed in the master bathroom, where the three 13 watt CFLs I substituted for three 60 watt incandescent bulbs were too bright. By unscrewing the middle bulb I found the lighting perfect, and I saved the $6.99 cost of one bulb.

If the equivalent CFL does not give you enough light, you can safely use the next highest wattage. For example, if a fixture warns you not to exceed 60 watts, remember that the equivalent 100 watt CFL uses only 26 watts. CFLs can be slightly longer than traditional bulbs, which could be a problem if bulbs are behind a tight glass or plastic cover. A lower wattage CFL will be shorter.

Use only dimming bulbs in dimming fixtures. Dimwit me, I put a regular CFL in a dimmer socket, and it promptly burned out, even though I never used the sliding dimmer switch.

CFLs take a few seconds to come on, and some require up to three minutes to achieve maximum illumination. So I kept the old bulbs over the only stairway in my house. Also I kept the old 75 watt incandescent in the overhead garage door opener, where a CFL would not work.

If your favorite store doesn't have the bulbs you want, try Home Depot or Costco, or Wal-Mart, which has made a commitment to sell lots of CFLs. Or buy online at: www.bulbs.com or www.1000bulbs.com. You can save money by ordering in bulk, but be warned that quality is not always the same when ordering online. The Energy Star label is an indication of quality.

What to do with old incandescent bulbs? The Habitat for Humanity outlet near my home accepted mine as donations. There are as yet no rules for recycling just a few CFLs; *Consumer Reports* suggests wrapping them in two plastic bags and placing them in the trash. (A CFL contains less than 1% of the mercury in a traditional thermometer.) If you have a business or a facility that uses lots of CFLs, go to www.epa.gov/bulbrecycling. Or try www.EasyPak.com. Or your trash collector may accept them: Waste Management does, for example, though it is costly for just the odd bulb or two (www.wmlamptracker.com).

What was my total cost? $218.93 for 30 CFLs at Ace Hardware. Sounds like a lot, but the Worldwatch Institute estimates savings between $50 and $135 per CFL over the four to nine years they last. At that rate I could save between $1,500 and $4,050, and the bulbs already paid for themselves during the early months of the first Obama administration.

Cynics, energy company lobbyists, even most politicians will tell you that converting to CFLs is not going to save the planet. They are correct in the strict sense that the energy savings and carbon reductions America must find cannot be achieved through CFLs alone. But those business-as-usual folks are not being honest. They are unwilling to change their wasteful ways, and they spend a great deal of money on lobbying, politicking, and public relations in order to prevent any changes. Defenders of an outmoded attitude toward energy, they ignore or try to belittle the most obvious environmental problems of our time.

First they tell us that global warming is hogwash, and the science supporting climate change is nonsense. When stubborn fact erodes the basis of that approach, they tell us alternative sources of energy will cost more, raising the price to consumers because the supply is not yet great enough. So increase the supply! Let there be government subsidies for fossil fuel producers to transition to alternative sources. Let there be mandated cost limits for energy, and financial incentives to do the research for cheaper technologies. But that's going to cost a lot of money, say the opponents, and finding that money will necessitate more borrowing and rising debt—as if the national debt had not been growing since the founding of the republic. Rising debt accompanies an expanding economy. It's not new debt we should fear: it's an unwillingness to consider new ideas. Besides, the costs of *not* addressing our environmental challenges will be even larger and will result in incalculable damage to the planet and all its peoples. Let's invest money in potential solutions, lots of them, that have a chance of getting the fossil-fuel monkey off our backs. But we will lose jobs, they moan, as if no one had ever lost a job, or had to retrain to find a new one. Successful economies alter priorities to meet changing conditions and encourage the deployment of labor and capital accordingly.

Some reactionaries are promoting the notion that we don't need new ideas, new technologies, or alternative sources of energy, because coal is cheap and abundant, and, best of all, coal is clean! But when you factor in the environmental and health problems that it creates, coal is certainly the most expensive source of energy. And what about the human cost of getting the coal out of the ground? Remember the twenty-nine miners killed in West Virginia during April 2010? Since 1884, *in West Virginia alone*, there have been 123 mine disasters involving nearly 2,700 victims, according to the state's Office of Miners' Health, Safety and Training (www.wvminesafety.org/disaster.htm). Although there has been a lot of talk about "clean coal," and some work has been done on demonstration projects, the reality is that clean coal is only a dream. It may never exist in meaningful quantities. Even assuming the industry could meet the technical challenges of creating a coal that did not pollute, and did not emit carbon into the atmosphere, it could not bring it to market for years. As Eric Pooley summarizes the situation (*The Climate War,* p. 301): "The coal industry was happily trapped inside a catch-22 of its own design. It opposed any mandatory reductions in CO2 until the day when carbon capture was commercially available, yet it was taking only minimal action to reach that day."

All of Pogo's "us" must wake up and realize that the fossil barons and their minions are stuck in a rut. That's why we need CFLs and green technology and green building codes and alternative energies, all of which will add up to a new industrial revolution. That's why the many people who have worked to create an awareness of environmental problems—a variety of writers, social scientists, public employees, church groups, community organizations, and volunteer associations—must keep on initiating effective local actions, not wait for government to get involved, or the fossil barons to see the light. That's why we need to rediscover conservation as a personal commitment and a way of life. What we need is not more stuff and continuous growth but a new world-view that moves away from Paul Bunyan capitalism and winner-grab-all takeovers. We need an ethic that embraces community, cooperation, and comity. And we need an appreciative, respectful approach to the natural world.

To fill those needs we must engender not just a new industrial revolution but an intellectual-cultural-spiritual revolution, something on the scale of the French Revolution that began in 1789 and eventually overthrew the rule of the nobles and clergy and carved a path toward representative forms of government, social and economic justice, and expanded options for all. That path is still far from a global super highway; it's not even a paved road in most parts of the world. In many places it remains a faint trail in the dirt. But the path is a way. Where it leads will not always be certain. But it leaves behind the smug shibboleths of the corporate mandarins, servants of a dysfunctional political economy.

What is a feasible way forward? One thing I've learned as a historian is that major events may be unpredictable in their outcomes, but are never inevitable in their origins. Leaders can make a difference, as can informed citizens. The difference they make is greater when both are working together, and when both are moving with the current of history, rather than against it.

Historians will differ about the direction and velocity of that stream, and about which tributaries contribute most to the larger current. What follows is my own assessment of how we can get out of the rut of outdated thinking and begin to work with a knowledge of the past to ameliorate our lot as humans. Americans must ramp up their involvement, but so must all nations, because the problems we face now are global. In outline form, our challenge, as I see it, is the following:

-to continue evolving away from kings, tyrants, and oligarchs of all sorts, and toward more representative forms of government that recognize the community as the ultimate sovereign;

-to continue evolving away from the politically fragile crutches of ethnicity, race, clan, or faction—while retaining respect for different cultural traditions—and toward real security, which is possible only when people are free and independent, and respect the right of all others to be the same;

-to continue evolving away from national exceptionalism, born of isolation and nourished by self-righteousness, and toward genuine participation in international affairs;

-to continue evolving away from a preemptory approach to foreigners, born of impatience and a lack of understanding, and toward a respect for difference and diversity;

-to continue evolving away from partisan, sectarian, regional, and short-term tactics, and toward long-term solutions benefitting everyone;

-to continue evolving away from quick fixes and toward a respect for the rule of law, the only reliable defender against ideologues and authoritarians;

-to continue evolving away from exclusive, intolerant beliefs based on myth and blind faith, often upheld by fear, and toward a spirituality based on recognition of how much we know, as well as on awe and curiosity for how much we do not know;

-to continue evolving away from rugged individualism, whose arrogant swagger did not even serve the pioneers who supposedly invented it, and toward a concept of the common good, embodied in the community;

-to continue evolving away from an outdated view of humankind as somehow separate from other creatures, and toward a recognition that all species, indeed all physical and chemical forms, are interrelated and interdependent;

-to continue evolving away from adolescent capitalism—the greatest engine for creating wealth ever discovered, but which is structured to favor the privileged—and toward mature capitalism, which has a conscience in its motors, so that distribution of wealth is more equitable;

-to continue evolving away from unsustainable development, and toward a new economics that accepts the realities of limited resources for the world's expanding population;

-to continue evolving away from an entitled mentality and toward a work ethic that made people prosperous in the first place—recognizing that we no longer have inexhaustible resources, and that we can no longer exploit what resources remain to us in the same unbridled fashion as we did before;

-to continue evolving away from mindless consuming and toward a discovery that such worthy goals as The American Dream, to be enduring, must consist of something more substantial than a rising net worth;

-to continue evolving away from the monuments of indifference and cynicism, raised through excessive self-regard, and toward the only pillars that have ever supported lasting happiness: love, concern for others, and participation in something bigger than one's self.

14. Attitudes 101

WRITING ABOUT COMPACT FLUORESCENT LIGHT bulbs got me thinking about other things one person can do that would make a difference for all of us. I could make a list for you, but many other people have already written entire books on the subject. The enormous quantity of information out there amazes me, but it also intimidates me. It would soon overwhelm even the most patient pilgrim, seeking the holy grail of environmental health. Which, in a reversal of expectations, causes us to feel guilty about what we are *not* doing, rather than proud of what we are doing.

The point is that books like that would not have been written, and people like you and me would not be reading them, if there were not already a huge desire to live and behave in a greener manner. Already more of us are driving fuel efficient cars, at lower speeds, and for fewer miles per year; more of us are eating fresh fruits and vegetables, buying more food in local markets, and shopping for fair-trade products and shade-grown coffee; more of us are conserving energy with efficient appliances, we are repairing rather than replacing, we are purchasing for value and durability, and we are recycling—all of which we do not just to save money, but also because it is the right thing to do.

Which really means that we are thinking differently. We are becoming more self-aware, and self-awareness includes the rational ability to consider the attitudes behind our thoughts. Just as a thought must precede an action, so an attitude certainly precedes a thought. Humans are thinking beings, happily so, but we are far too fond of our rational selves and woefully ignorant, often deliberately so, of the attitudes that drive our thoughts: desires, inclinations, urges, crazes, wants, yearnings, zests, hopes, wishes, dreams, fancies, imaginings, cravings, lusts, impulses, propensities, persuasions, proclivities, and passions. Some of these words may seem synonymous, but such a plethora of words illustrates the subtle differences between them, and the almost limitless range of enigmatic forces that squirm and wiggle and twitch and throb beneath the vulnerable veneer of our thoughts.

Now you're going to remind me about sex, money, and power—the all-too-evident troika driving our thoughts and actions. I acknowledge them. I know their power. But to focus only on The Big Three in the human landscape is to miss The Hidden Hundred that lurk everywhere in our unconscious.

It is The Hidden Hundred that give texture, color, and depth to the picture, that justify both our deepest despairs and our loftiest longings. We are more than our appetites. We are also an inspiring package of aspirations. Therein lies the breadth of our potential as a species, and your opportunity as an individual to make a difference.

Where do you start? Unless you are a dedicated loner, you will probably find the greatest scope for your talents within an organization of some kind. All such groups will need volunteers with diverse experience and abilities: computer skills, graphic design, grant writing, bookkeeping, program creation, office management, travel planning, membership development, publicity, and public relations.

My experiences as a fundraiser, a special-events coordinator, and a community relations coordinator have been useful to organizations where I volunteer. So are the many connections I've made over the years in the business world as an executive in the non-profit sector.

Almost any specialized or advanced education you have will be useful, whether applied directly like the psychologist who understands group behaviors, or introduced indirectly by the philosophy major who is accustomed to pondering different perspectives, or the historian who thinks about the influence of the past, or the artist who knows that esthetics is far more than style.

Any group needs a host of gofers, who are willing to drive, run errands, collate, answer phones, make phone calls, lick envelops, coordinate meetings, etc. Sometimes doing something well below your highest skill level can be refreshing. A good friend finds great satisfaction in working with homeless people once a week. Even more than such unskilled work, all groups need people with executive skills: organizing, planning, creating, synthesizing, analyzing. If you have ever been president or chairperson of a group, reflect on your experience. If you have not, perhaps now is the time. And I didn't intend to disparage the dedicated loners. Supporting all the visible activities of fundraisers, publicists, managers, and other out-reachers are good ideas, some of which will only occur to those solitary souls who like to sit and think.

Because I am so concerned about birds, I want to summarize their current struggle for existence, and include some suggestions for supporting them. In February 2009 the Audubon Society released "Birds and Climate Change." Based on records of the Christmas Bird Count across North America for the forty years 1966-2005, the report shows that large populations of all kinds of birds are moving much further north than usual to breed and raise their young (http://stateofthebirds.audubon.org). For instance, the green-winged teal has moved an average of 157 miles further north over that forty year period. Birds are moving further north because the climate is changing. Even in the first weeks of winter 177 of 305 species observed (58%) were found further north than during the same season forty years ago. Significantly, temperatures in January have risen more than 5 degrees Fahrenheit in the continental United States over those same forty years. Other reasons may account for some birds moving further north, but only global warming explains why so many of them are doing so. And more than birds are on the move, with ominous consequences.

Numerous scientific studies, based on long-term comparisons, have shown the disruptive effects of many species moving to higher latitudes and into higher elevations. The problem is, not all those on the move can survive. Think of habitat as a place to live. Consider niche as a way of making a living. Species must have both. And species don't live alone. They live in communities consisting of friends, rivals, and deadly enemies. Each community is adapted to such physical factors as temperature, moisture, soil content, wind, and sunlight, which compose a particular ecosystem.

So it's not just a matter of finding another habitat, but also a viable niche, among a suitable group of other animals, plants, and microbes, surrounded by a supportive ecosystem. Some species can change and adapt, if given enough time. But biodiversity has been declining steadily for the last 11,000 years, due to a variety of human activities, beginning with regular farming.

In March 2009 the Department of the Interior released its own "Report on Birds." It showed that in the previous forty years nearly a third of the more than 800 species in the United States have become endangered. (Updates can be found at www.stateofthebirds.org/) The details are even more alarming. Grassland species have declined by 40%, coastal species by 39%, and birds in arid lands by 30%. That represents hundreds of millions of birds.

The most distressing situation is in Hawaii. Nearly all birds there are endangered, and these species amount to about one-third of the American total. Humans and human activities are responsible. The scale of our cumulative impacts on habitats and natural processes has grown to the point that we have become a force of nature, and the same is true around the globe, not just in seriously threatened places like Hawaii.

So the bad news spreads well beyond birds. Birds are so-called "indicator species," which means that their health and prosperity, or lack of same, reveal the condition of many of the habitats where they live, habitats which are part of the many ecosystems that constitute the larger biosphere. If birds are in trouble, we are in trouble too, along with most other species on the planet.

The "Report on Birds" also found some good news. Conservation efforts have reversed the downward trend among many wetland birds, which have received a lot of attention. Of course, it depends on the species. American white pelicans, double-crested cormorants, and great blue herons, for example, seem to be doing well, perhaps even increasing in numbers, but American bitterns are decreasing, and the marvelous white-faced ibis teeters on the brink of trouble, its numbers fluctuating considerably from year to year. So before we celebrate the generally good news about wetland birds, let's consider the darker implications of this good news. Human impacts on bird species have become so deleterious—even if not deliberately intended—that doing harm is now the default result of human activities. Only when we choose to take redemptive actions can we save species, or ecosystems, or whole regions of the planet. Let's assume that we will choose to do so, and that we will increase the level of such activities. We have the ability. We have the resources. Do we have the will? Will we make it a priority to save birds, and the whole interconnected web of life of which we are an integral part?

Participating in programs that survey habitats and count birds is vital in generating information about avian populations and trends. On the national level this includes the Christmas Bird Count, the Breeding Bird Survey, and fun programs run by the Cornell Lab of Ornithology, such as Feeder Watch (www.birds.cornell.edu). Just recording the birds you see on your casual hikes and sending the results regularly to eBird is valuable (www.ebird.org).

Locally, in whatever part of the country you live, there are plenty of novel opportunities. Virtually every state has a Breeding Bird Atlas program, which uses volunteers to document all the birds that breed within specific blocks across the state. Many states have programs online that locate birds by county or along trails. Checklists of birds exist for most national wildlife refuges and state wildlife areas, but opportunities to create checklists exist for many state parks, open spaces, and birding hotspots. Asking around among your birding friends will disclose a surprising number of local efforts. For example, I am involved with a multiyear effort to study birds in the Bear Creek watershed of Colorado.

And remember, birding is just a start. Learning to identify species is satisfying, and knowing the name of a bird gives you a connection to that creature you lacked before. Next, you have the opportunity to increase your knowledge, and deepen your satisfaction, by going beyond listing to learn a particular bird's connections to other birds, plants, predators, prey species, and the whole network of life. Doing so will also enlarge your esthetic and spiritual appreciation of Nature, and introduce you to the beautiful and bountiful literature on birds.

Joining bird organizations or programs, and subscribing to bird magazines, gives those groups the financial and demographic support they need to do their jobs. One of my favorites, American Bird Conservancy, summarizes specific problem areas and what's being done, or not done. The details are often painful to read, but we need to know these things in order to take appropriate action. We can begin to turn things around by becoming informed, then contacting our legislators regarding specific bills, appearing at public meetings to make statements, even by writing letters and articles on conservation issues.

You can also help birds every time you visit the grocery store. Many of our familiar birds of spring and summer spend the winter in Central and South America, where they become vulnerable to a variety of pesticides sprayed on fruits and vegetables. One study reported that "a single application of . . . carbofuran can kill as many as 25 songbirds per acre" (*National Wildlife*, Dec./Jan. 2008). Most of these chemicals are banned in the United States, but not south of the border.

More and more chain groceries are carrying organic produce, which has not been exposed to chemicals. If your local store does not carry organic, try other stores that stock produce grown only in the United States, or try one of the specialty stores like Whole Foods, or your nearby farmers' markets. If you can't find organic fruits and vegetables in winter, consider doing without for that season. During our surge to abundance we became accustomed to eating fruits year-round that we used to enjoy only during summer. But our grandparents didn't have these winter luxuries; we can learn to live without them too.

Same with bananas and coffee. In traditional growing, both are exposed to lots of pesticides and fertilizers. But you can shop for organic bananas, and you can look for shade-grown coffee, both of which are grown under conditions favorable to birds.

Birds (and many other species) are in trouble because of our shortsighted obsession with material growth. That obsession impacts all the issues that worry nature advocates, from global warming to human population growth, energy development, resource extraction, pollution, land and water usage, and the extinction of species. Take a look at Audubon's "Birds and Climate Change" (www.audubon.org) for suggestions about participating in the solutions to these interrelated issues.

Because it is one of the least appreciated issues, I want to conclude this chapter with a summary on species extinction. In the normal course of events, some species disappear regularly (so-called background extinction), at a rate estimated to be one species every four years. (I'm talking about all species now, not just birds.) But in the last 100 years conservative estimates are that between 1,500 and 15,000 species have been going extinct every year. Other estimates (by no means the highest) are 30,000 a year, which would put us in the range of the five greatest mass extinctions of the past 440 million years, when, in each instance, at least 65% of all species disappeared.

Preserving species involves more than discovering a sentimental attachment to spotted owls or polar bears. Such poster species get a lot of attention, as they should, but focusing just on them distracts us from the many important reasons to appreciate biological diversity in general. Consider just three such reasons. Of the 250,000 known plant species, humans utilize a mere twenty to produce nearly all our agricultural crops, the bulk of which come from wheat, maize, corn, and rice. Disease, invasive species, habitat loss, and global warming are already making inroads on these essential foodstuffs. We may be able to find additional food resources among those thousands of other plant species, so it makes sense to preserve as many of them as possible. Second, natural species in their unmodified states account for over forty percent of our modern drugs; modified species contribute even more. Third, the more we understand other species, the closer we will come to grasping the mystery of life itself, including our own origin and evolution as humans. The more species we have, the more we will learn. We cannot afford to lose any more species.

As the dominant species on Earth, we have a responsibility to protect all forms of life. Surely, we want diverse fauna and flora, don't we? Enjoyment of wildlife and the natural world have always added quality of life to the human experience. It's time we started living within our means, so that other species can live too.

15. Open Space and Natural History

Remember the golden eagle, swooping into a valley beneath a high ridge in the San Juan Mountains of Colorado at nearly 13,00 feet? That's an example of what wilderness looks like. There are many views of wilderness, in a lot of different habitats and landscapes. According to the Wilderness Act of 1964, wilderness is a place "where the Earth and its community of life are untrammeled by man, where man himself is a visitor who does not remain." Open space is harder to pin down, but essentially it is a place that remains undeveloped. In a rural area, or a national forest, or on BLM lands, open space might qualify for wilderness status. Open spaces in or near cities rarely gain wilderness status, but they share a common purpose with wild places. By not allowing human infrastructure to intrude upon wilderness or open spaces, what is the Wilderness Act saying? It is *not* denigrating or in any way denying our splendid material and cultural achievements, but it is recognizing those proud achievements as only a part of our whole being.

Open space and wilderness areas remind me of humanity's origins and continuing place in the natural world. Yes, despite our many proud achievements, we are still a part of the natural world. We share a surprising number of genes with birds, beetles, even bacteria, indeed with all living creatures. All life is connected. All the resources humans have used to fashion our complex technology derive, directly or indirectly, from Nature's bounty.

To the extent that humans still love and appreciate the natural world, open space becomes a symbol and a means of connecting. Those connections are not just with land, water, animals, scenery and natural processes, but also with the spiritual dimension, however you define spiritual, and no matter whether you judge that life evolved from natural processes or from divine intervention. I believe that spirituality is an accomplice of consciousness, that both share a common origin we have yet to discover. Significantly, from the time early humans split off from chimpanzees, some six million years ago, they and their successors seem—based on the artifacts they created—to have assumed an intimate connection of spirituality with Nature.

We want and need open space for a variety of reasons. For relaxation and a temporary respite from our busy lives and many responsibilities. For the beauty of scenery, in all kinds of weather, and during all seasons. For the chance meeting with wild animals, with whom we have shared all of our previous history, some two hundred thousand years in the case of *Homo sapiens sapiens*—us.

Before continuing, let me deal with the elephant in the room: the shrill voice of practicality, screaming that the purpose of land is to be useful, to increase value! Yes, of course. But practicality is not everything. The land has a value beyond its use or its price. Land has always had an intangible value, indeed those nonmaterial qualities contribute to its dollar value. Increasingly communities are realizing that their open spaces and wilderness areas have a greater dollar value if left undeveloped. That is because numerous groups of humans—from hikers to hunters, bikers to birders, alpine and nordic skiers, lovers of space and solitude—bring their dollars to these places, primarily because these areas are open, pristine, untouched. The Fish and Wildlife Service found that Americans were spending $46 billion in a recent year to enjoy these outdoor uses.

Native Americans and all indigenous peoples have used land for the practical purposes of making a living, while simultaneously appreciating the spiritual, esthetic, and psychological dimensions of land. The concept of private property, while important in an economic sense, overlooks and diminishes those intangibles. So we need a balance: practical uses for making a living and intangible considerations for making a life. We need both, for without a meaningful life, making a living becomes mechanical and empty.

Maintaining that balance depends on making choices. And the choices we make depend on the questions we ask. What is the life we hope to sustain by making a living? What values are important to us? What do we want to accomplish during our brief time here? Addressing such questions infuses our lives with purpose, enabling us to rise above the basic struggle for existence. So let's choose for ourselves, instead of letting advertisers, salesmen, marketers, and the imagined pressure of peer groups impact our decisions. We matter. Our choices matter.

Making good choices involves reflecting on goals, establishing a plan, and exercising discipline. Those are the common sense virtues that historically Americans used to achieve their good fortune, but recently we seem to have forgotten them. We have been seduced into striving for comfort, convenience, and material gain, as if those luxuries would fulfill us. They don't. They merely fill the coffers of those who promote such addictions. Meanwhile, the reward for pursuing stuff and filling only our bellies, while neglecting our larger lives, has been loneliness, boredom, alienation, depression, rudeness, road rage, substance abuse, violence, and other demons of the age of gluttony.

From the back of the room, I now hear the whining voice of Jack Makemoney: "You tree huggers want to put us back to the Middle Ages. Don't you realize that material progress has made this country great?" Not to quibble, but in debating the gentleman, I would ask him to define "progress" and "great," and to consider the implications of unrestrained growth. But no, I don't want to revert to the lifestyle of a medieval peasant, and I believe a certain amount of material well-being is a good thing— provided it does not overwhelm other values.

What does all this have to do with open space and natural history? Not much, just everything. Open space reminds us of our deep connections to Nature, it symbolizes our appreciation for intangible values, it reinforces our understanding of community, for all species thrive in conditions of diversity and choice.

Here's an exercise that I guarantee will uplift your life, especially if you practice it regularly. Go take a walk in your favorite park or open space.

As you stretch your muscles, expand your imagination. Observe your surroundings, noticing how little the furniture of the landscape depends on humankind, yet how much we depend on it. Drink in the scenery. Contemplate whatever creatures you encounter, including other humans.

Notice the impact this dance with Nature has on your mind, your body, your spirit. Some psychologists equate this kind of exercise with therapy. Gurus would say it is the gateway to enlightenment. New Age folk call it centering. Some religions find the basis of miracles here. What it boils down to is you reconnecting with your deepest, truest self by noticing and appreciating the natural world around you—all of it, from the pulsing life in the soil beneath your feet way out to the farthest star you can imagine.

16. South Table Mountain: Summer

JULY 14, HIGH SUMMER ON the grasslands atop STM. My day begins at the base of the mesa, admiring its silhouette jutting into the clear blue sky. By rights, STM should be a wildlife refuge. Open space now claims two-thirds of the mesa, and it is unique among all the "properties" of Jefferson County Open Space in terms of its wildlife. Those of us who come here have little impact on the land, and that is partly because we respect it and want to preserve its mystical dimension of place. Ironically, we know the land better than the "owners," who cling to an archaic sense of place as possession, or the "managers," who, like bean counters, can put a price on something without grasping any sense of its value. Sadly, it is those who never come here that have the largest impact on the land, and their obsession with paperwork, planning, and property aims only to create another homogenized product.

I love this place, and I appreciate the mesa and its present ecology more by putting it into the perspective of deep time. At the base of the mesa one finds sandstones hundreds of millions of years old that contain numerous fossils, many of animals now extinct. Scores of those creatures swam in ancient oceans that several times engulfed the region. During dry intervals when the ocean retreated, dinosaurs roamed here.

An awareness of past extinctions triggers thoughts of my own inevitable demise. But wandering around STM, where I have learned to see myself as part of the landscape, I find consolation, indeed inspiration, in knowing that life itself is resilient and resourceful. While I and all other friends and species I know will pass away, the steady flow of life goes on, mutating into other forms, adapting to new places and styles of survival. "There is grandeur in this view of life," and it is satisfying to realize that my thoughts travel some of the same paths once trod by Charles Darwin.

As I tramp around the mesa, I often wish Mr. Darwin or some other formidable teacher could accompany me. I am an eager but all-too-amateur naturalist. I know so little about what I see and discover. What are these graceful yellow flowers? How do they relate to the brambles next to them, and to the insects that crawl on them, or the birds that flutter over them? How many insect species can live here? Are the birds the dominant order in this special place, as I suspect? Such questions constantly overwhelm my ability to answer them. I resort to libraries and books, where I find valuable nuggets, but I lack the experience, the intuitive grasp that only comes from years of dedicated searching, to exploit the deeper veins of knowledge. Alas, my serious matriculation in the school of Nature occurred years too late.

One thing I know: STM is an extraordinary place. Though mostly flat, and entirely surrounded by the maw of Denver, steadily swallowing the countryside, there are swales here that, once you wander into them, make you think you are lost in some rural corner of Kansas, or perhaps Oz. Fringed sage, Fendler senecio, evening primrose, wild alyssum, wild rose, indian paintbrush, and numerous sunflowers blossom here. Native grasses such as blue grama, needle-and-thread, and big bluestem still flow in erratic currents, though a casual observer will more readily notice the yucca, the prickly pear cactus, the sentinel-like mullein, and the widespread cheat grass. Happily, and as a testament to the regenerative power of the native flora, the invasive weeds account for only a small fraction of the many plants that grow here: my friend Loraine Yeatts counted 436 species of plants on South and North Table Mountains, over a period of eighteen years.

As the flora testify, this is dry country. Technically it is classified as semiarid, but on a hot summer day it is desperately dry, crispy dry, the kind of dry that warps the leaves of skunkbrush and splotches yellow the porous skins of cacti, like a cancer cannibalizing the photosynthetic, life-enhancing green. Even the grasses, as recently as ten days ago a hopeful kelly green, have now reconciled themselves to a stoic tan. Rabbitbrush stands firm, stout, wispy strong, boasting of its adaptability, but every growing plant here could use a soaking rain. It hasn't rained in weeks, and the exuberance of early spring, the temporary lushness, has vanished. Even imperturbable lichen, growing everywhere on the volcanic outcrops, looks more brittle than usual. Within minutes a good rain would restore its vitality.

My first route today follows the canal at the base of the northwestern slope. Because of the rising temperature, animals are already taking cover. Mule deer have descended to the cooler slopes and hide among the scrub oak or the mountain mahogany. Foxes and coyotes have denned up. Even flies are subdued; a couple give me a faint-hearted pass. Mosquitoes are nowhere to be found. A bumblebee cruises slowly and efficiently from one flower head to another, enjoying more nectar than he is storing. Only grasshoppers buzz and graze with any enthusiasm, impervious to the heat and sensitive solely to a demonic inner turmoil.

The birds are quiet. Most have found some shady refuge where neither feathers nor calls give them away. Along the canal only a few birds move about. A family of Bullock's orioles crop some shrubs, the parents instructing their young. Yellow warblers dance among trees beside the water. Above the canal, in the dry slopes, I spot the bird of the day—a Lazuli bunting, with his dazzling blue head, large white wing bar, rufous chest and white belly. He snags insects off the shrubs, in and out of which he disappears and appears like a fairy in a technicolor dream.

After walking the canal, I drive around to the west side of STM in order to ascend a wide ravine. Two chatty women start up the path just ahead of me, one adorned in a red bonnet that is right out of a Camille Corot landscape. The shrubs soon absorb their voices. A jogger nods as he descends. Part way up the slope, several western kingbirds chase and flirt. Flickers gobble up ants along the trail. Higher still, near the rim, a single spotted towhee pops up to sing. From the way he glares at me, I know he does not worry about a rival; nor does he seek companionship. He's letting me know, in the time-honored way of prey species, that he sees me, thus depriving me of the surprise that is the predator's greatest advantage.

The towhee reminds me of its cousin, the green-tailed towhee, who also favors the shrubs. A less robust bird—possibly a more finicky eater, certainly less abundant in this place—I suspect the green-tails may be losing out in the struggle for niche. I have not seen them for the past two years. I used to know two locations where they nested. No longer. Perhaps, hopefully, they have eluded me, but I fear the worst.

As I reach the top of the mesa, it is nine o'clock and already feels like the inside of an oven. Avian life seems even scarcer up here. Partly this is due to geography. The mesa's top is essentially flat and open, depriving even the stealthiest stalker of any advantage. Shrubs around the periphery give me only a temporary blind. Mountain mahogany, for example, a colonial breeder on the slopes, becomes a more solitary pioneer once it reaches the mesa, spreading out, then soon disappearing amid the ocean of grasses. On the bare branch of a Chinese elm sits a female American kestrel. I see nothing that might encourage her to burn off a few calories in the hope of ingesting a few more. Apparently, neither does she. She turns her head to take notice of me, perhaps 200 yards away, then turns away, obviously unconcerned.

Another raptor, a golden eagle, perches on the high beam of a power pole, the wires of which extend across the mesa, north to south. It sits about a quarter of a mile away, and I intend to walk right beneath this bird. I try to walk nonchalantly toward the tower, but I am curious to see if this majestic creature will tolerate me or take wing. The eagles nest along the north slope of the mountain, and I have often watched them, from a considerable distance, in various stages of breeding.

With its superb vision, probably ten times more powerful than mine, this eagle can probably count the whiskers on my unshaven face. If familiarity breeds anything more than contempt, I suspect the eagle will recognize me, not as a denizen of this place, but as a frequent and unthreatening visitor. In what I used to think was the silly and wholly unscientific manner of humans, I propose the following hypothesis: if the bird stays put, it shows that he (she?) recognizes me, which will make my day. The hypothesis is not so silly, because careful testing has shown that crows can recognize individual humans. Remember that prairie falcon that used me as a beater? Perhaps he did so because he recognized me as a creature who walked through shrubs, who might thereby stir up a meal.

Perhaps the eagle can also make use of me. As I walk along an old road I occasionally stir up four-legged eagle food. In the event, the eagle stays put, giving me a smile, and I wander on in search of sage thrashers.

Mercifully, clouds have now spread across part of the sky, screening me from the sun and dropping the temperature by several degrees. A breeze picks up. It is lazy, its breath is warm, but in moving the air across my skin it cools me—somewhat. Swallows, mostly cliffs but a few barns, scour the air lanes overhead, proving that insects are here, too, though I have sensed few of them. A lone vesper sparrow fills the hot dry air with musical trills so convincing that my neurons immediately bring up the memory of *Aida*, performed at the Baths of Caraculla in Rome fifty-four years ago. But I can't remember what I had for supper last night. I'm hungry now, having staggered out of the house this morning at dawn without taking breakfast.

Western meadowlarks, highly territorial and so abundant and vociferous in spring that I can count a separate pair almost every fifty yards, have transformed themselves from beautiful singers and bold performers to clucking skulkers. There are chicks to be raised and fed now, and most of that work can be done along the ground. There is little need to fly.

Having completed my loop route, I turn west and begin to head down. I reflect how few humans I have seen today. Corot's model and her friend have disappeared. Two girls jog along a distant trail. A cyclist stops as we meet (a rare occurrence), to ask what I've seen, the binocular hanging from my neck providing his clue. We talk amiably about the eagle, which he had not noticed. Though absorbed in our own private purposes, we humans fit comfortably into the landscape. Each of us has come here knowing it is a place where we belong. We come as pilgrims to a shrine, refreshed by the space, rejoicing in the solitude, renewed by the rediscovery that we are more than our puny, perishable selves.

17. Attitudes 301

I WANT TO START THIS ESSAY by quoting my favorite Dilbert cartoon (author Scott Adams, May 10, 2000).

> Dilbert: "This product would melt the polar ice caps and doom humanity."
> Coworker: "That's okay."
> Dilbert: "You're part of humanity."
> Coworker: "No, I'm in marketing."
> Dilbert: "I won't help you destroy the planet."
> Coworker: "That's what I said until I saw the free T-shirts."

I'll bet the farm you had a good laugh at that! I still do, every time I read it. My copy of this cartoon sits under a plastic pad on my desk, along with other favorites. But after chuckling at the absurdity of the coworker's position, there is a serious point worth pondering. "No, I'm in marketing" is a wonderful cop-out, isn't it? I don't run the world, I'm just in marketing. Or sales. Or accounting. Or development. Or construction. Or banking. Or engineering. Or law. Or medicine. Or shipping. Or inventory. Whatever.

It's not your fault that the world is going to hell. No, not entirely. But you abet that process if you think of yourself only as your job. Part of being human is belonging to a network of connections, from family and Girl Scouts to employee, citizen, representative of our species, and inhabitant of our planet. We are not fully human unless we acknowledge our many community memberships and act accordingly. That may sound like a platitude, but it is something I learned the hard way. I was not always fond of community. I was not always a nature advocate, despite my lifelong love of birds and the outdoors. Many small events and circumstances, and some influential friends, helped move me along. I cannot acknowledge them all here, but I will mention the single most powerful stimulant that led to my changed attitudes.

At the age of twenty my son put a pistol to his head and pulled the trigger. He totally surprised me, his mother, his sister, his girl friend, and all who knew him. He devastated all of us. Even if you have never experienced anything quite like this, you can imagine our feelings: the shock, horror, disbelief, desolation, grief, and guilt. None of his survivors were culpable in his tragedy, yet all of us were linked to him, all of us were somehow a part of the circumstances against which he so desperately reacted, and none of us had the foresight to see what was coming.

Even before Henry's death I had been gradually moving away from the loner status I had evolved as a teenager to cope with an uncertain world and unreliable people. Gradually, I found comfort in connections as I gained confidence in myself and enjoyed some worldly success. Birds had a lot to do with my new outlook, largely because watching birds and learning of their many links in the natural world made me painfully aware of how many ties I was missing. Henry's death made me appreciate more keenly and practice more diligently the reciprocal duties of friendship. It has been a long and uneven journey, which is far from complete. One of the things I learned is that not everyone can be my friend. Some people simply do not mix; others stir up antagonistic bile. Best to avoid them. That may be a sad conclusion, but it is based on the way things are.

My appreciation of connection and community are genuine, but that appreciation came at a price. My hope is that my experience, some of what I have learned about the natural world, can bring you the benefits of connection without paying the price of painful dislocation. An awareness of community stimulates a shift of attitudes that leads to healthy connection.

No, it's not my fault that the world is going to hell, but I cannot help feeling somewhat responsible. The collective impact of all of us, in our jobs and in all the other small ways we impact Mother Earth, is enormous but mostly invisible. As I begin to grasp the huge outlines of that impact, a chilling rain drops on my soul. At that point it would be easy to walk away, to raise my own umbrella and seek the quiet shelter of home. But looking through the gloom to see a brighter picture is possible. Getting involved in some local project joins me to the millions acting all around the world, each in their own small way. That provides tonic for the soul.

But it is amazing how easily I slip back into bad habits and attitudes. Not long ago I imagined having a different belt for each pair of trousers I owned. No more having to pull a belt out of the loops anchoring it to one pair of trousers, then guiding it through the loops of another pair of trousers, being careful not to miss any loops in the back, where I can't see them. How tiresome!

But honestly, all those belts would not have added an iota to my happiness, and who would have noticed anyway? What appalled me was realizing how potent is the impulse to act in the service of convenience. Yet this is a common vulnerability in our consumer economy.

When I was in graduate school, a long time ago, my first wife and I learned with astonishment that our combined incomes placed us below "the poverty level." We laughed a lot about that, and we had fun reminding our affluent friends working downtown on Wall Street of our many deprivations. Yes, it was fun because we lacked for nothing we needed and enjoyed a busy and rewarding lifestyle.

Rather than making us poor, being frugal gives us choices, makes us aware of values. The trouble with affluence is that you can never have enough stuff, yet, as we keep learning, stuff doesn't make us happy. Back in the 1970s I took the *Est* training, and during a discussion of abundance the trainer asked each of us to write down on a piece of paper how much money we needed, and how much we wanted. The slips were collected. One gentleman stood up to say he could not distinguish between need and want, and he found it impossible to put a dollar figure on either. The trainer encouraged him to ponder how much money he would need to feel satisfied, and to share again once he had resolved his dilemma. Some time later, the gentleman stood again to announce that the only amount of money that would satisfy him would be "all of it." There's the dilemma of material things in a nutshell. It's not that things are bad in and of themselves; it's that things are not fulfilling, satisfying, conducive to happiness, because they are only things.

Despite the problems threatening all natural systems, and therefore threatening us, too, I am encouraged to realize that many, perhaps most, of those problems can begin to be solved by viewing them from a community perspective. For example, to the extent that we have an "energy crisis," it is not in our dependence on foreign sources, or even in the world's dwindling supply of petroleum, or the polluting effects of oil spills and burning coal. Those real problems stem from our over dependence on fossil fuels. But the crisis derives from our absurd attitude that maintaining a wasteful, inefficient, unsustainable, and, yes, immoral lifestyle is good for us, something to which we are entitled.

Such thinking has blinded us to our connections to all other peoples, all other creatures, all other life forms. Such thinking has poisoned the wells of conscience, broken the bonds of community, trivialized philanthropy, and belittled altruism. Worst of all, such thinking has pumped up our bloodlust for scapegoats, making it difficult to consider where and how we might be responsible.

As I've aged, I've come to understand the wisdom of the notion, inherent in many traditional cultures, that tribal elders should summon up their courage and speak out regarding the lessons they have learned. But as I've weighed my observations, more than once I have had to confront the various Biblical injunctions against criticizing others until I have truly reformed myself. Not casting the first stone, for example, or failing to see the beam in my own eye.

Again, a shift in perspective makes all the difference. The Biblical injunctions, the parables, the many stories and proverbs, all those inspiring messages, were not written for genuine saints, whose numbers have always been miniscule. Those counsels of perfection were conceived and uttered, then later recorded, for ordinary citizens like you and me, real people, imperfect people, who mostly want to do the right thing but who are constantly tempted to do otherwise.

Thinking about repairing or recycling provides another opportunity to shift attitudes. Some people fear that having to fix or recycle might start them down the slippery slope to budgets, planning, savings, or, what is worse, frugality. Frugality makes them feel poor, or makes them fear that things are scarce, whereas affluence makes them feel rich and secure in the illusion that they will never run out of anything they may want, including things way beyond their reach. But even if you are rich, there's a limit to how much you can buy, use, eat, display, or store away.

Previously, in Attitudes 101, I discussed the improbable fact that even you, just one individual, can make a difference. The conclusion of Attitudes 301 seems even more unlikely: that unless you act, nothing will happen. It seems a portentous conclusion, but if you think about it the logic is inescapable, mainly in considering your role as a leader. When leaders dawdle, communities, organizations, nations, whole continents can fall asleep.

So what can you do? The canyon of possibility stretches before you, threatening to swallow you in its vastness. To find the path of discovery requires courage, independence, resourcefulness, and pluck. Mostly, it requires original ideas—a vision. That's what leaders provide.

Sooner or later, anyone working for Mother Nature at a leadership level is going to have to hold her/his nose and dive into the sewer of politics. The stink keeps many good people away from politics, which is a shame, because the odor emanates mostly from the camp followers—the money grubbers, the pimps, the fixers, the vested interests, and the smalltime Charlies—who see in politics only an opportunity to advance themselves. They care nothing for the common good.

But politics also attracts others leaders and idealists, who have visions of their own. They embrace politics because anything that impacts public policy is ultimately political, and it's the political solutions that can make a big difference. An excuse good people use for not getting involved is that "everything has become political." Actually, the reverse is true: what we have too much of today is partisanship, and too little politics. Partisanship is posturing. It is essentially irresponsible, for it aims only to justify and promote its own narrow self-interest.

Here we arrive at the real challenge, for politics provides no silver bullet. Politics is only the art of the possible. Its success depends upon patience, compromise, and integrity. We cannot rely only on political solutions, no matter how sweeping. Before, during, and after political efforts, we need a personal attitude that inspires and orients our lives. That's the vision. With vision, we can reform our ineffective politics, redirect the potent tools of our economy, and revise our wasteful habits.

Of all forms of government, democracy is the slowest, the most inefficient, the least predictable, and the most frustrating. Its chief virtue is that it values diversity, choice, and opportunity. Tyrants and their ilk care only for themselves. Elitists put themselves on a pedestal because of greater wealth or other advantages. Only democracy provides the means of achieving lasting benefits for the common good. When confronted with global problems, only democracy recognizes that all of us, regardless of our different conditions, abilities, and imagined superiorities, are in the same boat, that only by cooperating can any of us hope to prevail.

Wealth and power won't protect the fortunate few from the effects of overpopulation, pollution, and global warming. At best, the rich and powerful might live a little longer, in increasingly dangerous and appalling conditions. Is that the best *Homo sapiens* can do? Is that all you want? If not, you need to get involved in politics at some level.

You don't have to run for office to be involved in politics. You need to care fervently about something (it will grow out of your vision) and be willing to work with others. Does your municipality recycle trash? Would you like to see higher fuel economy standards for vehicles? Would you like to see your community expand its public transportation? How about motivating contractors to "build green"? Do you want to increase biodiversity? Save habitats for wildlife? Reduce invasive species? If you don't have a favorite cause, just pick one. Your passion will grow as your investment increases.

An issues campaign will likely provide greater scope for your imagination, but it will also challenge your versatility. Don't try to do everything. Or, at the other extreme, as Roger Pulwarty, a climate scientist at NOAA (National Oceanic and Atmospheric Administration), says: "Don't let your inability to do everything be an excuse to do nothing." At the same time, don't become too specialized. Everyone loves to catch a long pass, but everyone must be willing to confront the problem galloping directly at them. A solid tackle can be as satisfying as a glorious romp.

Regardless of your job description, your role as a leader is to see and act on opportunities. Sometimes that will be addressing an expressed need: "Who is the best link to each of our supporters?" Sometimes the most pressing need has not yet been acknowledged: perhaps your directors need to take a weekend retreat and rethink their approach.

If it sounds like there are more races to run than you have horses, you are right. That's why leaders are rare, and that's why you put them (i.e., you) in the toughest races.

18. Leaves Are Us

WHILE FISHING NEAR A BRIDGE spanning Bear Creek, and listening to the gentle current gurgle beneath me, I imagine this modest stream carrying its loamy load of creatures and bouncy baggage of stuff all the way to the Gulf of Mexico. The experience reminds me of a book I read as a child, *Paddle to the Sea*, which told the adventures of a small canoe, carved by a boy who placed it in a stream bound for the ocean. Bear Creek begins at Summit Lake, beneath Mount Evans, in north central Colorado, and it has already visited four life zones by the time it passes this obscure bridge in an urban park just east of the town of Morrison. I too have wandered through many habitats of those four life zones along Bear Creek, mostly while looking for birds, so I feel a kinship with the stream. It has just completed a splashy, swift descent of the foothills; now it catches its breath, slackens its pace, and smoothes its stride as it enters the plains and prepares to merge with the South Platte, just as I did a few weeks ago in a larger canoe.

It is autumn. Many are the treasures this stealthy creek has purloined from the surrounding land, none more beautiful or more vulnerable than the multi-colored leaves, kidnapped from their parents and now delivering a living ransom to a greedy undertaker. Some shimmer in the light like sparkles in a girl's hair, still brightly colored as they float along the surface. Others shrivel, become splotchy, and begin to disintegrate as they sink into the flow. Red, yellow, brown, green—including many shades of each— even spots of black, all are beautiful in their spiraling dance.

Leaves find different ways of traveling along the current. Each reminds me of varying ways I have met the challenges of life's stream. Some rush down the center, following the main flow, but these racers rarely pause to notice their surroundings or to contemplate their journey. Others, more exploratory, swirl with an eddy, drift by a bank, linger for a time in a backwater, or stall on a snag. Still others plunge to the depths, often catching hold of something that temporarily arrests their inevitable recession.

Taking home a cottonwood leaf to examine under a magnifying lens, I find common patterns in the epidermis of the leaf and in the skin of my own arm, patterns that resemble plots of fenced land as seen from an airplane. Were I able to look even deeper, with the aid of an electron microscope, I would find a cellular structure that, if placed beside a specimen of my own cells, would be difficult to distinguish. Yes, the leaf is distinct in employing chlorophyll, its tissues are reinforced with lignin, and it depends on chloroplasts to manufacture proteins, but both I and the leaf have many similar organelles in our cells, including ribosomes, mitochondria, rough and smooth endoplasmic reticula, and Golgi bodies, not to mention various vesicles, membranes, microtubules, a nucleus, and DNA.

Both leaves and humans are vessels of nutrients. Our internal organs specialize in the circulation and absorption of those substances. Our internal structures reflect the ways we each have adapted to collecting those same nutriments. Thus the leaf stretches an external skin into a giant canvas on which the sun, the air, and the elements paint their intentions, while my skeleton, muscles, and tendons cooperate so that the whole bag of bones can cavort and gather my necessities. Both humans and leaves depend largely on water, oxygen, nitrogen, and carbon, and, regardless of how proudly I may later perform my appointed tasks, I and all humans sprouted from groupings of tiny molecules into complex multicellular organisms, and so do leaves. All of us grow inexorably, reach and surpass several stages of maturity, and attempt to recreate a part of ourselves in the next generation. And we all die.

We humans would seem to be the greater players on life's vainglorious stage. But consider how many of our roles are only more elaborate, perhaps frivolous, ways of growing, metabolizing, reproducing, and dying. And consider how much of what leaves and we do is programmed by our genes, and how many of those genes we share in common with leaves. Leaves are us. We are leaves. Not precisely or completely, of course, but in more than a metaphoric sense. We all descend from bacteria, in the short run of a few billion years, and, in the longer term, from exploding supernovae and from the original Big Bang itself.

Pondering that makes me reflect on the humbling variety of life. By 2001 scientists had counted around 1.8 million species on Planet Earth. Including those yet uncounted, total estimates of earthly species now range from 3 million to over 100 million. Did all this squirming, teeming mass of life evolve from just one exploding star? Or was our primeval gaseous soup a product of many such explosions? In any case, given the billions of known galaxies in the universe (and allowing for how many more there might be), there is plenty of reason to assume multiple life systems out there, some connected to ours by the proximity of cosmography, others perhaps by the tentacles of super octopuses.

Life flows like a stream; it carries portions of all that is and all that ever was. The leaves spinning beneath the bridge at Bear Creek Lake Park approach the last stage of existence, at least in their present form. A worm will eat particles of a leaf, a fish will swallow the worm, the fisherman will hook then eat the fish. Fragments of the fisherman, eventually reduced to dust, will spread across the land, erode into a drainage, and flow to a pond, at the edge of which root hairs of a tree will absorb his dissolved mineral ions to nourish its leaves.

19. The Beauty *Is* the Beast

IN ADDITION TO BEING A naturalist, I am also a humanist, meaning that I treasure the unique abilities and accomplishments of human beings. Some thinkers argue that it is not possible to be both at once, just as some of my former college faculty colleagues thought that it was not possible to be an original research scholar and an inspiring teacher at the same time. I disagree, but the controversy is of more than academic interest. At issue is whether people of different skills and professional training can find sufficient mutuality to solve problems impacting both scientists and humanists—and all the rest of us along with them.

I am encouraged to think that they can. Scientists like Edward O. Wilson, Carl Zimmer, or the late Stephen J. Gould have a solid grounding in the arts and humanities, just as literary figures like Peter Matthiessen, Barbara Kingsolver, or Gary Snyder have a deep appreciation for the role of science in our modern society.

One of the chief problems on the world's agenda today is agreeing on the nature of Nature. Does Nature include humans, as well as all creatures great and small? Or as Protagoras—the fifth century B.C. Greek philosopher, grammarian, and orator—seemed to imply when he said "Man is the measure of all things," is man separate from Nature? Because neither the original context nor the intent of Protagoras' remark are clear, we can leave him out of the argument, but his words have echoed down through the ages with disturbing implications for naturalists, whose experience tells them that humans are part of Nature.

Failing to acknowledge the connectedness of all life, and the staggering diversity it has evolved, postpones the day when humans will strive to live in harmony with their physical surroundings, when they will finally realize that by harming Nature they sabotage themselves. Put another way, only when humans grasp our intimate connection with the natural world will we start appreciating the many free services provided by the world's many ecosystems, which in turn make possible our survival and prosperity. In 1997 the annual value of those services was estimated at some 33 trillion dollars, which, if nothing else, makes a powerful argument for preserving biodiversity. Put in local terms, Tadini Bacigalupi, a sociology professor, has calculated the annual value (during 2008) of Nature's services at $4.6 billion in just one national forest of Colorado (the Pike-San Isabel).

However short-sighted, anthropocentric, silly, or just plain wrong the notion of separation may be, the idea boasts an impressive pedigree. For instance, it has long enjoyed a widespread currency in economic theory, geopolitical planning, and military strategy. It lay deep in the unconscious assumptions of the civilization that grew from the ashes of the Roman Empire, and it stimulated the rationalists who wrought the Scientific Revolution of the seventeenth century, just as it throbbed at the heart of those entrepreneurs who initiated the Industrial Revolution of the eighteenth. Both capitalism and socialism subsequently endorsed the notion of separation of humans from Nature. The Judeo-Christian world view has always seen humans as only partly physical: because they partake of the divine through spirit, or soul, humans uncouple from Nature in some essential though mysterious manner. Only in the lifetimes of those now alive has science itself grasped the linkages between all life and the universal applicability of the laws of physics, chemistry, and evolution to all matter and all life.

The notion that man is the measure of all things suggests a number of interesting implications: that man is really the *only* judge of all things, including himself; that man, restricted to the standard of himself, is incapable of understanding much else besides himself, if even that; that man's understanding may be limited to measurement; that measurement is not the same as understanding. And so on. But on none of these issues do I wish to dwell.

What provokes me are four essential questions. What is man, according to man? What does man think of Nature? What might Nature think of man? And how might mankind avoid the dreadful consequences of accepting the solipsism that man is the measure of all things?

So what is man, according to man? My view is that man is a mixed bag, equipped with marvelous talents but also devious tendencies, superb vision but horrible biases, high ideals but corruptible habits. I am not alone in that view. For some of the poetry of language, as well as some of the deep insights, let me draw on two great literary figures to illustrate the dualistic nature of man's being. In *Hamlet* Shakespeare puts the following words into the mouth of his self-conflicted protagonist:

> What a piece of work is a man!
> How noble in reason!
> How infinite in faculty!
> In form and moving how express and admirable!
> In action how like an angel!
> In apprehension how like a god!

But Blaise Pascal in his *Pensées* expresses a different view.

> What a chimera then is man!
> What a novelty!
> What a monster, what a chaos, what a contradiction,
> What a prodigy!
> Judge of all things, feeble worm of the earth,
> Depository of truth, a sink of uncertainty and error,
> The glory and shame of the universe.

One finds such diverse appraisals throughout literature. Perhaps all our arts are nothing more, and nothing less, than a vast, vainglorious self-commentary. Captured in such artistic renderings is the complex character of humankind: not all bad, not all good, but a fascinating mix of each.

Consider some famous examples. Before becoming a father of the Christian Church, St. Paul was a brutal bigot. St. Augustine, by his own confession, indulged his yearning for sensuality. Though a creative theologian, John Calvin was a self-righteous tyrant. Picasso could be cruel, especially to those close to him. Because they can be both diverse and perverse, individuals display wide variety in what it means to be human. To think of George Washington is to conjure up an entirely different universe from that of George W. Bush.

My favorite example is Wolfgang Amadeus Mozart, whom many consider the highest expression of musical genius who ever lived. But Mozart aptly illustrates that talent spreads indiscriminately across the range of human character and personality. Mozart was an ambitious self-aggrandizer, a man who disobeyed his patron, the archbishop of Salzburg, humiliated his own father (though Leopold certainly deserved it), scorned the taste of Emperor Joseph II, and created, with relish, a group of string quartets that he knew would puzzle and overshadow Franz Joseph Haydn, his only musical peer.

The moral dualism we see in ourselves carries over into our traditional attitude toward Nature. Thus we divide Nature into what is good (useful or pleasant for us) and bad (harmful or too exotic for us). Out of laziness or arrogance, we tend to assign other creatures to a kind of background, over there, with us safely separated from them, over here. Notice the self-serving logic at work in such thinking: it is acceptable for humans to be diverse, indeed variety accentuates our glory, yet diversity in Nature presents inconvenience, resists predictability, poses danger. Thus for nearly all of human history, we have viewed Nature from a self-referential and self-serving focus, never doubting that we were a superior, progressive species, entitled to tinker with our physical surroundings, and to "manage" any of the other species in it.

How did we arrive at such a myopic viewpoint? By taking our own PR too seriously. For generations anthropologists and archeologists have been telling us how wonderfully different we are. Lately they've been joined by cultural historians and evolutionary biologists. We've celebrated ourselves because of erect posture, manual dexterity, tools, big brains, language, and culture—without considering the side effects of such gifts.

Among those side effects would be the numerous wars we have waged with each other; the number of species we have driven to extinction; the many "primitive" peoples we have extirpated; the amount of damage we have done, and are doing, to the ecosystems that support all life. Considering how much of the Earth's land mass humans monopolize for our own purposes (over half), we begin to look like a universal parasite.

Our grandiose assumptions about ourselves have also blinded us to our own vulnerabilities. Recently, we have learned that automobiles, industrial production, and clearing of forests have impacts on climate change, with many damaging effects on human health. We are only beginning to grasp that tiny mutations in our genetic code produce surprising results. For example, people who have evolved an immunity to malaria are more vulnerable to sickle cell anemia. Chimpanzees and humans have an almost identical genome, yet when exposed to the AIDS virus, chimps are immune to the resulting complications, whereas we get sick: at least 25 million of us have died, another 50 million are infected, and two million more are dying each year.

But now that humans are beginning to discover a different view of Nature, and of our own place in it, it is time to ask some different questions. How do you suppose other creatures interpret the world in which they live? And what role do they see for themselves in it? How might they view us? To even imagine such questions demands a perspective that is utterly unfamiliar to humans. Of course, we assume our pets and other domesticated animals have feelings. Also we tend to attribute human characteristics to the "higher" primates (instead of considering how much of our humanness has evolved from primates). However, it is a stretch for most of us to imagine that other creatures might have consciousness, and therefore easy to dismiss questions about how other critters view us or their physical surroundings.

Research into consciousness plods along at the horse-and-buggy stage, and it generates heated controversy. We still cannot define what we are talking about, or where to find it, or how to activate it. But some scientists already think diverse creatures have consciousness. Eventually, I predict, research will disclose that consciousness—like thought, language, and intelligence—is an evolving attribute that has a history and will be discovered in other creatures, and, what may be more surprising, it has a future too, which means that it is not a static state, not a clear destination, but rather a station along the way. Elucidating consciousness may be analogous to a microbe's wanderings along the whorls of a conch shell, winding and twisting and roaming its way across time and space without ever reaching a terminus.

Let's take another slant on the issue. Assume for a moment that bacteria had consciousness too. What would their PR folks say? They would proclaim how adept they were at exchanging DNA and improving their immunity, how versatile they were in adapting to every known habitat, how prolific in spawning countless varieties. They would remind us that bacteria have been around for over three billion years, *Homo sapiens* for roughly two hundred thousand. In that time, a few bacteria have created great havoc, but the overwhelming majority have found beneficial employment: dissolving wastes, including toxic wastes, digesting grasses for herbivores, and processing food for virtually all mammals including humans. There are many more bacteria than cells in our bodies, and scientists are just beginning to grasp the fundamental link between bacteria and human health. Moreover, bacteria convert gaseous nitrogen to a form usable by countless creatures, they assist in photosynthesis and recycling carbon, and they promote the growth of roots in trees. Not bad for a mere microorganism!

Looking at the comparable track record of humans, I am left with some troubling questions. Are our achievements tied in some way to a heedless disregard of consequences? Is it part of our essence that whatever we imagine we feel compelled to attempt? Is dominion over other creatures incompatible with responsible stewardship? Do we have choice in such matters, or is the will to power more than an aberration? Is it, perhaps, the defining character of our species?

Given the performance of our species so far, I am inclined to answer "yes" to each of those questions. But I think there are grounds for expecting change. Why do I think so, given the persistent obtuseness and knavery of a vocal portion of humanity? Because humans are more than conniving opportunists. Humans are capable of lucid thought, objective decisions, big-picture perspective, and unselfish behavior. Because the accumulation of knowledge is a progressive endeavor, despite the imperfect nature and retrograde tendencies of some who gather it. Because the connectedness of species, the unity of humans with Nature, is more than a biological reality: it is also a powerful and potentially transforming idea. If the human species survives, it will almost certainly do so because it evolves into a more tolerant and cooperative one, one that understands and respects the similarities of all life. Is it possible that we might move in that direction?

It is encouraging in this regard to reflect on the history of ideas. Old beliefs die hard, but eventually persuasive evidence has a way of winning the day by sweeping away old mythologies. Once upon a time people believed Earth stood at the center of the universe, with the sun and all other heavenly bodies revolving around it. Those same people believed that the visible stars in the sky floated within a perfect crystalline sphere. Despite the solid work of such astronomers as Copernicus, Brahe, Kepler, and Galileo, it required centuries to overthrow such nonsense.

More recently, some people have believed that mankind was a unique and special creation, exempt from the laws of physics, chemistry, and evolution that governed other lesser creatures. But paleoanthropologists have now identified at least twenty different hominids, or early humans in the family of man. At the very least such discoveries raise questions about what it means to be human. More pointedly, they undermine beliefs about the specialness of our creation. In the fullness of time I think evolution, natural selection, and the connectedness of species—which Darwin proposed so convincingly a mere century and a half ago—will become as commonplace as heliocentric thought, a spherical Earth, or universal gravitation, each of which was once unthinkable or unacceptable.

My perceptions tell me this is so. My perceptions are a product of all the experiences I have endured and all the intuitions that guide me. My perceptions are knowledge-based, not faith-based, and they tell me that life on Planet Earth, as well as all the physical structures that define it and all the chemical compounds that nourish it, are part of an integrated, holistic system—perhaps like Gaia, if Gaia is more than a metaphor. Or perhaps like a potpourri, or a mandala. Maybe like a grain of sand.

20. The Ties That Bind

SOMETIMES I GET SO GLOOMY that I feel isolated, and I believe my petty life doesn't matter. I have felt that way any number of times. When my parents died prematurely. When my son took his own life. When I quarreled with a friend or loved one. When I confronted prostate cancer. I live alone, for the most part happily, but there are times when I wish I did not. There are plenty of occasions for this kind of grief. We all know them. I notice all these griefs have in common my lacking or losing a connection.

On the other side of the happiness coin are some of my solo triumphs: becoming a champion swimmer as a teenager, graduating from Yale, earning a Ph. D., climbing all the fourteen-thousand-foot peaks in Colorado, reading every volume of the collected works of Sigmund Freud, and romancing a number of beautiful, accomplished women. I don't regret any of those splendid experiences. They were fun, educational, and became part of who I am. But it is revealing how these individual deeds satisfy me less than what I've accomplished with others: with other faculty and graduate students, creating "Racism and Prejudice," a course for Stanford University that was the first step in establishing a program and a department of Black Studies at that university; with fellow members of the Colorado Mountain Club, implementing a large and successful program of outdoor recreation and education; with members of a local Audubon Society, creating an imaginative bird monitoring program; serving as an executive officer with three non-profit groups, and with several others as a volunteer. And, looking further back, connecting with my beloved grandmother through the broad-tailed hummingbird. Thus, for me, the greatest happiness has been equated with connection.

But there are times when it is necessary to be alone. Borrowing a page from the Stoics's book of philosophy, I find a consoling side to an unwanted solitude. I call it the view from outer space. From whatever distant star or galaxy I might imagine, the challenges of my life on Planet Earth amount to very little from that faraway place. I find this positive because it weighs the small turmoils of my individual self against the larger gyrations of the universe. A more pitiless way of arriving at the same mood is to imagine life ten million years ago. Back then humans didn't matter because we had not yet evolved. Imagine life without our hyper-inflated self-importance. Yet life did very well indeed without us, for over three billion years, and it will do as well again in another ten million years, long after we have passed from center stage.

But consolation or ultimate fate aside, we are alive now, though briefly, and we do matter. We matter to ourselves because we have this sometimes merciless, sometimes glorifying self-consciousness. And we matter to others because we exist in a seamless web of connections. Even an unrepentant criminal dwelling in solitary confinement is never alone. He has his jailers who watch him, cooks who feed him, administrators, social workers, and statisticians who keep track of him, lawyers, judges, and witnesses who have put him where he is, and may now be reassessing his circumstances in order to release him. And he had, probably still has, a family, or the remnants of one, that partly shaped him and is partly responsible for his present dilemma, not to mention the teachers, employers, companions, and assorted other individuals who crossed his path, however briefly, and had an impact, however small. Like it or not, we are rarely truly alone.

And never truly independent. Socially, we are everywhere and always connected to others, mostly unconsciously, and effective action is merely the deliberate mobilization of connections. Compared to all other life forms, human beings are most successfully defined by the potential of their social connections. More than what we eat or what we achieve, even more than what we think, we are the sum of our connections, beginning before birth and extending throughout our lives. We cannot survive alone. Individuals are fascinating in their variety and in their differing skills and experience, yet individuals matter most when they are plural, not just singular.

Thinking about that for a moment brings me to the unsettling realization that it is probably impossible to know clearly who I am. As humans we experience a constantly changing set of circumstances. We are links to others past and present, threads in the larger web of life, itself constantly changing, and fragments in a tumultuous universe. The only identifiable self is that body we walk around in, yet it varies from meal to meal, day to day, menstrual period to psychic state, sickness to health, and from mood to mood.

Which brings me back to attitudes. To a large extent, I am what I chose to be. Considering all the chaos and upheaval I face, exercising that choice is a necessity, if I hope to create a viable identity. Despite the fact that any such self-definition may consist of big doses of hope and fantasy, our own self-sense provides our only constant, and from that partly mythic foundation we source our sanity, orient our purpose, launch our activities, and become whom we choose to be.

Even after arriving at some acceptable, practical sense of self, the many interactions we cannot escape constantly challenge our self definition. Others see us differently than we see ourselves. We will be contradicted or derailed by the expectations of others, whether justly or not. The ties that bind can also impede or even strangle, if we let them. It's a matter of attitude.

Another difficulty facing individuals is that corporations, governments, or churches—and other such organizations—can pursue stupid or immoral or even illegal policies while giving cover to the many individuals they employ. Individuals in such groups can hide behind institutional procedures, allowing them to duck responsibility, but few of them will have good feelings about their employment.

Corporations in pursuit of profits can lose sight of the larger common interest among the places and people where they do business. The American auto industry is a case in point. Despite the growing market share of small, more fuel-efficient cars imported since the 1960s, The Big Three in Detroit ignored this trend and ballyhooed for larger, less efficient cars, claiming that's what the public wanted. Wrong! What Detroit wanted were the larger profits available from those gas guzzlers, and the energy industry went along for the ride.

Yes, Americans bought SUVs, and other fuelish cars before SUVs came along, because for over forty years The Big Three has successfully lobbied Congress not to increase the fuel tax, thus persuading Congress to subsidize inefficiency and shortsightedness. By 2006, despite the best efforts of Detroit to the contrary, Americans were buying more foreign imports than domestically produced cars. That should have been a wake-up call, but Detroit snored on and did not awake until the collapse of the auto market in 2008, as part of the worldwide recession.

Wall Street is the symbol of our nation's financial system, and on its integrity depends the credit of the nation. Too often, however, Wall Street gets caught fouling its own nest, as in the Bernard Madoff scandal of 2008. Such scandals now spread internationally in a New York minute, as Robert Allen Stanford's frauds proved in the same year. Far worse than these periodic scandals, however, has been the reluctance of large financial institutions to reform the very practices that led to the global meltdown in 2008. That financial hotshots were encouraged to conjure up a bizarre and confusing array of schemes to enrich themselves—usually without the supervision of senior officers, who often failed to understand the clever debt instruments they approved—makes American businessmen look like opportunistic predators, rather than the providers of opportunity they claim to be.

Governments can get bogged down in group-think, as President Lyndon Baines Johnson's cabinet demonstrated during the Viet Nam War, or as the administration of the second President Bush so brilliantly proved in Iraq. Churches can lose the distinction between dogma and reality. My favorite example among many is the Catholic Church's prosecution of Galileo Galilei for heresy in 1632. Galileo was both the keenest observer and the deepest thinker of his era. It took three-and-a-half centuries for the Church to acknowledge its error.

How do we liberate individuals from these mental prisons? By reminding them that corporations, governments, churches, and all other organizations are abstractions; only the people in them are real. Despite their awesome buildings and monuments, their huge budgets and bureaucracies, their hoary traditions and shiny symbols, all institutions are the invention of individual humans. Organizations cannot survive without the dedication and imagination of those individuals, yet individuals will eventually lose their identities, which is to say their souls, unless they stay true to themselves by not allowing organizations to subsume them under cover of ideology. Of course, this raises delicate problems of loyalty and employment, but also ones of justice and morality. Alert humans are exquisitely qualified to make such choices. Again, we are more whole when connected, but only if our connections are freely chosen, mutually fulfilling, and based on integrity.

We are more than our jobs or careers, or even the many roles we assume during our lives. Because of our intricate and overlapping connections, what we do impacts all the rest of us, whether we act alone, in groups, or on behalf of large institutions. As individuals we are each distinct in delightful and difficult ways, but we are more alike than different. Alone we reach the peaks of glory or the pits of despair. Together we can make a difference.

So are we individuals? Or are we units of a larger social and ecological order? Of course, we are both, constantly and always. The difference is priority. Nature consumers, I suspect, give the priority to our particular differences: our birth, status, wealth, nationality, religion, ethnicity, ability, ambitions, and achievements. While recognizing our differences in all those respects, nature lovers and advocates give priority to our similarities: how connected we are through strands of DNA, how constrained by the laws of physics, chemistry, and evolution, how linked through our different societies, cultures, and civilizations to the greater unity of human potential.

So, yes, I am a nature lover, and also an advocate for Nature, for my priority is to preserve and protect her. That doesn't make me better than someone else whose priority is more self-oriented. Nor does it justify someone else scorning me for being different from them. We must get beyond such petty morality, which bears a huge responsibility for keeping us separate, in hostile camps of self-righteousness. Let's get back to connecting with Nature and community. That is what the ancient Greek philosophers meant by virtue: devoting one's self to fulfilling the common good. I particularly like the Stoic slant on virtue, which is to strive to be the best we can be, given our circumstances, always keeping the community in mind, and never to renounce that which makes us human: reason. Yes, reason, the tool of our thinking selves; reason, the override button that can suppress or redirect those sometimes nasty impulses arising out of our emotions; reason, the means, perhaps the only sensible means, by which we can change our attitudes.

In the past century, and still today, reason has suffered many defeats at the hands of barbarous thugs. Regimes have been altered for the purpose of destroying alleged enemies. Clans, ethnic groups, religious sects, whole nations have been whipped up into furious hatred by vicious ideologues. Such well-known atrocities have accompanied, even defined, the so-called modern world. Yet aggression against each other is futile: no single group of us can ever overwhelm all others. Wars and terrorist tactics between groups will only weaken the ties that bind. Dominating and sabotaging each other within groups will eventually destroy those ties. The goal of the many different peoples of the Earth must be to rediscover the wonders of Nature and our mutual links to her. Only by realizing our common heritage through Mother Nature will we direct our intelligence to protecting her, which will redeem us in the process.

A more subtle yet equally toxic force has been the increase of rudeness, the deliberate scorning of civility by those who have raised their individualism to a new form of pathology. Think about the neighbor who allows his dog to stay out all night barking, or who makes no attempt to pick up the poop the mutt has deposited on your lawn. Or the driver who takes up two parking spaces, or cuts you off as he/she changes lanes at highs speed. Or those who allow a door to slam in your face, who butts in line ahead of you at the movies or the grocery store, who fails to return calls or follow up on promises. Such petty acts are rude, inconsiderate, or lacking in common sense, or all the above, and they are spreading like a virus throughout society. Reason and the bonds of community, our appreciation of a common humanity, have declined accordingly. So far has this insidious process advanced that the only way we can now reverse it is to wake up and realize that neither clever irony nor super cool promote community.

How can we counter the hostile acts of our inflated egos? Essentially by re-establishing the ties between individuals and community. Individuals come together for protection, for mutual advantage, and to encourage clan, family, and person to flourish within an identified community. Philosophers and statesmen since ancient times have known that individual genius cannot flourish, or even be recognized, without a supportive context. Where would Socrates be without his polis? Where would Michelangelo be without his papal patrons, or a philosophy we know as the Renaissance? Where Einstein without Newton, modern mathematics, and quantum mechanics?

Behind all these communal achievements have been the many cultures that have created them, reflecting the diversity of values, beliefs, and behaviors that both define and delimit what it means to be human. The complexity and variety of human behaviors can seem bewildering, even threatening to those outside a particular membership, but the multiplicity can be managed, and the exotic tolerated, by realizing that behind the diversity are different answers to the same essential questions. Among them: How shall we live? What do we value? Whom do we respect? At the heart of any society are groups of individuals who have agreed upon answers to the basic questions.

From our diversity have emerged impressive examples of creativity in action. We have brought into being imaginative literatures, original art, probing philosophies, brilliant self-appraisals, as well as the libraries, museums, and universities to nourish and preserve these gifts—all fashioned in numerous languages and by countless cultures. We have created laws that illustrate the extent of our intellect, and traditions that show our spiritual resourcefulness. We have built cities that demonstrate our ingenuity as well as our esthetic sensitivity. The potential and diversity of human creativity is a source of wonder. But as transportation shrinks physical distances, and as populations swell beyond sustainability, the need for revitalized cooperation is growing—if we are to avoid what Thomas Hobbes called "the State of Nature," in which were found "no arts, no letters, no society, and, which is worst of all, continual fear and danger of violent death, and the life of man solitary, poor, nasty, brutish, and short."

The ancient Greeks were not alone in connecting virtue with community.

A common element in all ethical systems is that same respectful concern for others. All faiths and major philosophies seem to recognize the social duties and bonds that make us human. So if that be virtue, let's have more of it! Virtue has endured a bad press from time to time. It has been confused with the prissy starchiness of the puritan, the arrogance of the self-made man, or the self-righteousness of the zealot. It is none of those narrow bigotries, for by its nature it is inclusive. In the end humans cooperate not because it is virtuous to do so, but because it is practical. It is the way to get things done, especially when different beliefs and traditions must be accommodated. Cooperating to achieve results for the common good is virtue in action.

21. South Table Mountain: Autumn

Aᴜɢᴜsᴛ 30, ᴀ Sᴀᴛᴜʀᴅᴀʏ, sᴛɪʟʟ a number of days from the Autumnal Equinox—not the most obvious date to choose for a fall bird count, but I have my reasons. It's 7:00 o'clock, and as I park the car I think about sliding into a light jacket, to bolster the meager insulation of my T-shirt. I stuff it into my knapsack, assuming from the clear sky that the sun will soon warm the chilly air, but I'm glad to be wearing long trousers.

I begin my ascent of the mesa on a well-worn trail, which pushes up the north slope rather steeply from just above the Rolling Hills Country Club. I've ascended this route scores of times, and I'm hoping to find a number of old friends. Just as I expected, a rufous-sided towhee jumps to the top of a shrub to challenge me. I can't help thinking, although it is an example of mankind's tendency to humanize creatures, that this bird is actually rising to greet me. After all, I have seen him (or her: the females look the same) in this same shrub dozens of times before. Or have I? It could be the mate, or a sibling, or a rival who has displaced the original tenant, or even a youngster who has inherited the estate. Still, for the first bird of the morning to be a species that has often appeared before in the same location is a great consolation.

Continuity is comforting, which is why I have never fully accepted the decision of the American Ornithological Union to change the name of this perfectly named bird to spotted towhee. Oh, yes, I understand the scientific reasons: another rufous-sider living in a different region of the country has attained full species status, thus the presence or absence

125

of those white spots have become diagnostic. Hence, eastern towhee and spotted towhee. How drab! Why not let the unspotted congener retain the original name of rufous-sided towhee?

In quick succession, as I puff up the trail, I encounter still more old friends, each in the expected locations: a western scrub jay barks as it skims along the shrub tops. American goldfinches graze on the seeds of a mullein patch. A rock wren calls from cliffs overhead, then two of them descend and show themselves in the grass. I whistle for the canyon wren, but at this season he's not going to bother returning my feeble imitation. A red-tailed hawk, having just dived on a prey, and missed, now embraces a rising current of warm air to rise gracefully to 200 feet where it lingers, circling, searching, blending with the sky, gradually disappearing in the fashion of soaring raptors. Best of all, I startle a great horned owl from a shrubby ledge among low cliffs; it flies to another favorite perch 100 yards away and almost disappears in the wall of a steep escarpment. Had I not followed his flight and watched his landing, I could not locate him now, so perfectly is he camouflaged by the surrounding colors, uneven angles, and undulating forms of the cliff. I'm pretty certain I know this bird. I used to live below STM, and in winter he roosted in a locust tree in my front yard during daylight hours. During and after breeding season, he and his consort prefer these more remote crags.

Yes, continuity is consoling and comforting. But the unexpected lurks everywhere. Broad-tailed hummingbirds always delight in displaying their aerodynamic skills, and in spring they confine their enthusiasm to each other, focused as they are on the ardent business of breeding. But in a few brief months youngsters have grown from tyros to tyrants. Now they launch from shrubs, rocket into the sky, duel with each other, then descend to harass and intimidate whatever moves, including me. Rivalry between species is especially fierce. A female rufous hummingbird, tiny but titanic in temperament, charges all comers: a bee, a jay, other hummers, even a mule deer that dares to munch a succulent flower.

Menace stalks the air. A Cooper's hawk swoops over the shrubbery, hunting a meal, disturbing a pair of kestrels that quickly hustle this intruder out of their territory. They take turns intersecting the hawk, herding it ever higher, away from the trees where they may have youngsters, finally forcing the larger accipiter up and over the cliffs and onto the grasslands atop the mesa. Moments later the kestrels do their own menacing. The female chases a mourning dove off a wire; the male pursues some unseen prey in the shrubbery beneath the tree where they nested, only to be attacked by that same rufous hummingbird. I am the fortunate observer—amused, surprised, enthralled—who has the pleasure of watching this life-and-death drama from a safe seat in the lower orchestra.

Of all the seasons none involves more drama than fall. Consider the name itself: fall, the time when leaves fall off trees, when the length of days is falling from its summer peak toward lowly winter solstice. Metaphorically, it is the decline and fall of summer. Biologically, it is the decline of metabolism toward its lowest sustainable level, reached well before the onset of winter on December 22.

But what of autumn? Though the word has assumed the essence of ripeness, and suggests the maturity of crops, it is a puzzler. The Oxford English Dictionary assures me of its uncertain origin. I like that. A little uncertainty about quite certain phenomena is a good thing. Going way out on a limb here, I assume that the Latin scholar who first coined the word had in mind not so much ripeness or decline as metamorphosis—change. The word autumn goes back via the old French *autompne* to the Latin *autumnus*. Who first coined the word? I want to believe it was Ovid, the witty Roman poet of eroticism, who collected some of the best myths of the ancient world into a long narrative poem, called *Metamorphoses*. In it he described, among other wonders, how a woman was transformed into a bird. In fact Ovid narrates numerous such changes: the sisters of Meleager turned into guinea-hens, Scylla into a shearwater, and the nine daughters of Euippe into magpies. I fantasize that the lively rufous hummingbird of STM resulted from a similar alteration.

At any rate, fall (autumn) best embodies the season of change. Summer boasts of steady growth. Winter embarks on a solemn sleep. Spring doesn't change so much as it erupts, and it moves, like summer, in only one direction. Autumn goes back and forth between growth and decline. A September snow can nearly destroy your garden, while an October rain can partially revive it, even prolong it into a late Indian Summer of November.

What primarily intrigues me is the timing of autumn. From previous experience I know that autumnal changes begin well before September 22, the official start of the season. So let's consider the varying evidence I gathered on August 30th for the onset of autumn, or seasonal transformation. Remember that rufous hummingbird? She wouldn't think of being in central Colorado unless she was already migrating. At the moment she's in the midst of a 2,500 mile voyage, en route from southern Alaska to Mexico, where she'll spend the winter. Say's phoebes certainly nest in nearby parts of Colorado, but I have only seen them here during autumn, on their way to Arizona and parts south. Today I find one in the grasslands atop the mesa; he's using a fence post as his watch tower, from which he spots insects then sallies out to snap them up.

And then a rare treat: I spy a burrowing owl on the periphery of a prairie dog town. Likely, there are more, but I only see one. Normally, I would approach with great stealth, secrete myself beneath the lone tree overlooking the town, and scan the area hopefully for owls. I have only seen this migrant twice in over fifteen years, both times during autumn. This time, having seen the owl without half trying, I am so delighted that I decide not to sneak in and search for more. Probably, there are others, but finding one is quite sufficient.

Why are these owls so scarce? After deep contemplation and no research, I decide that burrowing owls probably travel like we do, stopping at places offering more food, security, even comfort. Think of motel chains. Why stay at Motel 6 if you can afford Holiday Inn? So I suspect the habitat at STM is equivalent to about a Super 8: you only stay there if better places have no vacancy.

While noticing these travelers on the move, I am even more struck by those who have already moved out: vesper sparrow, Brewer's sparrow, sage thrasher, blue-gray gnatcatcher, gray catbird, yellow-breasted chat—all summer residents and local breeders, and all gone. Interestingly, the winter residents who share the same niches, but in different seasons, have not yet taken up residence. As yet, no rough-legged hawk, no northern shrike, no mountain chickadee, no white-crowned sparrow.

What does this tell me about the territory? Obviously, it no longer suits some birds, nor does it yet suit others. Which makes me think that maybe the timing of migration depends less on the quality or location of the territory than on the different evolutionary histories of different species. Some are adapted to prey on particular critters that are becoming scarce at STM (these have departed), while others are adapted to feed on critters that are still plentiful elsewhere, somewhere north of here (these have not yet arrived).

But what of the other migrants: the additional flycatchers, the vireos, nuthatches, kinglets, bluebirds and warblers? No sign of them yet. Does that mean they've already passed through, while I wasn't looking, or have they not yet arrived? And what about a flock of other birds—blackbirds, meadowlarks, kingbirds, swallows—that are still here but will depart any day now. How long will they stay? So many questions, so little time!

Pondering arrival and departure dates makes me consider the state of the vegetation. The flora also display signs of irregular transition. Willows, Russian olives, cottonwoods, and the solitary Chinese elms, escapees from ornamental gardens below, remain mostly green, still sucking in sunlight and converting it to carbohydrates. Some leaves of mountain mahogany are already turning, and the distinctive curly, feathered seed heads have been ready to go for weeks. Yucca have gone even further: about half the sword-like leaves still show a pale green, the rest a dull blond. Other cacti have all finished flowering, as have virtually all the forbs; I find only one species of aster and one of sunflower still in bloom. The various grasses, now exhausted and reduced to the appearance of straw, have closed their photosynthetic factories and poured their remaining energies into their seeds, which are now dry, brittle, loosely attached, ready to fall or blow in the wind.

Not so the rabbitbrush, whose seeds remain firm and waxy. Still cloaked in a vibrant chartreuse, this vigorous plant seems indifferent to the aridity of its surroundings. Viewed in clumps across the grassland, rabbitbrush remind me of tanks crossing a desert—squat and defiant, but at the same time vibrant and luscious. Several invasive species still attract pollinators: numerous yellow thistles, still unguentary, several Dalmatian toadflax, and a scattering of bindweed along the roads.

Bindweed illustrates the importance of habitat. Here, controlled by a dense carpet of grasses and forbs, bindweed can only grow where humans have scraped the soil sufficiently to disturb the natural enemies of bindweed. In my yard, however, the feeble Kentucky bluegrass yields readily to the ubiquitous bindweed—a testament to the vigor of wild plants at STM.

Insects and other invertebrates give the same mixed testimony regarding the onset of autumn. Ants no longer swarm over their hills. On the great majority of sites I inspect, only a few stragglers crawl around, the rest presumably prepare for winter underground. Grasshoppers have lost their vitality. A couple of weeks ago they jumped clear of me long before I could have squashed them. Now they remain anchored to the ground as I approach, seeming to invite their demise. I resolve to avoid them, preferring to save the fresh meat for my avian friends. Butterflies, normally abundant in summer, have mostly disappeared. In over four hours of exploring I find exactly two, perhaps monarchs or viceroys, in any case skittish and eager to avoid me.

Other invertebrates seem oblivious to the changes ahead. Flies, bees, and wasps still patrol, dragonflies still perform their helicopteral dance, and dung beetles plod along, clumsily crossing the terrain with no apparent plan or success.

Before descending the long slope to the place I've parked my car, I pause to relieve myself at the edge of the sweeping grassland. Any creature that looked my way could see me, but the only one that might embarrass me is nowhere to be seen. Ah, the sweetness of solitude! Yet I am not alone. Beside a still-green plant, where I deliver my nutrients, is a mostly deserted ant hill, on top of which a coyote has delivered a turd. A message if ever I saw one. In the right circumstances my liquid donation might also be interpreted as a message. But the ants ignore both deposits, demonstrating, perhaps, the superior judgment of colonial dwellers: they don't have time to acknowledge such acts of individual bravado.

Beginning my descent, I pause again beneath a stunning work of natural art. Countless species of lichen stretch across the cliffs, most of them gray-green or yellow-green, or a brilliant sulfur. Amid all the change stands this symbol of the eternal. It is always there. It thrives in all seasons. Yet the more I look at this complicated symbiont, the more I wonder how it, too, changes from summer to fall, from winter to spring. It certainly grows, but does it also contract, does it change its color, or alter its form? I must watch more carefully, more often.

Still more questions, and no immediate answers. I could return at different intervals during autumn, and I will, but the few answers I may have unearthed by the time I return will only raise more questions. Only one answer seems satisfying for autumn: this magical season does not conform comfortably to human calendars. The date we agree upon stems from an acceptable astronomical reference, but Nature knows no such convenience. This arbitrary stellar calculation tells us nothing of seasonal progression or intensity. To experience that, you would want to visit the same place every day between late August and late November. Only then would you find autumn in all her glorious and unpredictable variety.

Before my final descent, I'm hoping to see the rufous hummingbird again. So beautiful, so zesty, so full of life, yet declining across the West. No luck. My memory obliges with a remembrance of two different hummers in the canyon lands of Colorado, some ten years ago. I was surveying a BLM tract to ascertain if it qualified as wilderness. I had been up since dawn, and I was pooped. I was lying down, flat on my back, trying to escape the summer sun under one of the few trees in the vicinity. I actually fell asleep. Not sure how long I slept, but a distinct buzzing sound awakened me. It seemed to be right on top of me. Fearing I had collapsed near the nest of wasps or some other hymenopter, I opened my eyes but resolved not to move too suddenly. What I observed astonished me. Two broad-tailed hummingbirds took turns circling over me. In between rounds, they perched together on a branch above me and seemed to confer, looking at each other, then at me, raising and lowering their swords, uncertain whether to impale or salute me. A couple of times they both descended simultaneously, dropping close to my face, then circled up and hovered, all the while looking at me then over to each other. I was wearing nothing red, which attracts hummers. No honey or anything sweet stained my clothing. So far as I know, hummers do not feast on dead bodies. The experience lasted some five minutes, and ended when I decided to slowly raise myself to a sitting position. Apparently this satisfied their curiosity, and they flew off.

Go figure. I have never heard of a similar encounter with hummers, but it reminded me of something. Birds have more sensitivity and intelligence than we allow them. Had I been living in classical Greece, I would have interpreted this visitation as a message from the gods. Indeed mythology contains countless stories regarding intimate encounters between animals and humans, which tells me that in our sometimes overly empirical approach to phenomena we may be missing obvious clues to reality, clues that speak to our intuition.

I believe those hummers were reminding me that all life is connected, and that all life intuitively knows it is connected. That essential insight has been with me ever since I watched hummingbirds nest from my perch atop a toilet seat, and conversed with robins from the branches of an apple tree. I didn't know where I belonged then, but I sensed that birds might be my mentors. After following them a while, I learned that birds conjoin in a ring of life and that I belonged to a human fellowship with ties to that ring. I knew this from an early age, in the way that you know something without knowing that you know it. Birds helped to deepen an awareness I already possessed.

But humans have helped too. Ironically, the fickle wheel of fortune, or in this case misfortune, played a large role in the next stage of my connecting. Learning that I had prostate cancer in the spring of 2008 proved to be a blessing in disguise, first as a boon to my writing. Several essays in this book found their first expression after I got the bad news, which sharpened my awareness of myself, my surroundings, and the fragility of life itself. Even better, I opened up more to people, including those family members and friends who had gone AWOL at the time of Henry's death. One of the sadder things I learned from his death, then again at the time of my cancer, is that some people are simply not able to reach out when others are in crisis. Death and disease can make normal relations awkward, of course, and people fear saying or doing the wrong thing. But in such circumstances the only mistake is to say nothing. I appreciated deeply a simple acknowledgment of the situation, but I was puzzled and, yes, hurt that some people who could have reached out did not do so.

But the best result of confronting the cancer was finding a deep reservoir of genuine caring available to me. It overwhelmed me, and at first I felt that I didn't deserve such an outpouring. Eventually, I realized we all deserve love. It isn't something you have to earn. It has a peculiar rebounding quality in that the more you give away, the more comes back to you. The cancer has been treated. It will be a while before I know how successfully. Cancer has a nasty habit of sneaking back, even after being dormant for years, but thanks to modern science I am well into my third year as a cancer survivor.

Acknowledgments

MANY FRIENDS, FAMILY MEMBERS, AND colleagues made a big difference in bringing this book to fruition. The following offered comments, criticism, or encouragement, sometimes a bit of each, after reading earlier versions of these essays: Dan Allen, Mary Evers Allen, Terry Andrews, Ruth Arendt, Dave Balogh, Bob Bethel, the late Bill Brockner, Fran Corsello, Jim Derby, Peter Dessauer, Peggy Durham, Patty Echelmeyer, Fran Enright, Warren Finch, Everly Fleischer, Iris Fontera, Michael Friedman, Barbara Jean Gard, Maryanne Gilbert, Brwyn Harris Downing, Mike Henwood, Sid Hollister, Veronica Holt, Matt Jackson, Gail Laughlin, Alice Levine, Norm Lewis, Barbara Ludwig, Meredith McBurney, Margaret McDole, Marlene Merrrill, Liz Moore, Michele Foster Oakes, Tina Poe Obermeier, Patti O'Neall, Sue Osborn, Mary Parker, Graham Phipps, Sheila Ray Duranso, Jay Reed, Paula Reed, Bob Righter, Deborah Roberts, Libby Roberts, Sylvia Robertson, Warren Roske, Niña Routh, Jean Smith, Jane Stewart, Cynthia Tamny, Lois Harlamert Teegarden, Terry Vogel, Jim Wade, and Sally White.

Heartfelt thanks go out to those who sustained my spirits during a difficult health challenge, which happened to be the time I wrote most of these essays. A number of these wonderful people also offered valuable commentary on one or more of the essays, and because I have named them above I will not repeat their names. The others are Michele Aldrich, Ted Ames, Brad Andres and Heather Johnson, Lyle Baker, Jim and Audrey Benedict, Sylvia Brockner, Karel Buckley, Darla Chase, Chuck Clement, Lee and Nell Cliff, Terry Combs, Sheila Daly, Tom Daly, Ardeth Daly Donaldson, Bill and Joan Eden, Dr. James Fagelson, Joan Daly Francis, Leslie Gerard, Dr. John Hedberg, Tim Hogen, Don King, Jackie Lawrence, Jim and Nancy McClelland, Kay Niyo, Ron MacArtney, Dick Prickett, John Richards, Erik Roberts, Mel Ryan-Roberts, Terry Romero, Jack and Ruth Salter, Dr. David Schreiber, Dr. William Shipley, Bill Studier,

Carolyn Vachani, Dr. Gordon Vineyard, Ron Welch, Bud and Juanita Weare, Sherman Wing, and Shawheen Young.

For exceptional caring I want to recognize and thank Michele Foster Oakes, Maryanne Gilbert, Gordon Vineyard, and especially Sheila Ray Duranso, my Florence Nightingale and good friend. For continuing to share her wisdom in matters literary and editorial, as she did with my last book, I thank Alice Levine. For being my muse and perceptive critic over the final drafts of this book I joyfully acknowledge Brwyn Harris Downing.

Select Bibliography

Bergman, Charles. "A Rose is [Not] a Rose," *Audubon*, January/February 2008.

Braasch, Gary. *Earth Under Fire: How Global Warming Is Changing the World*. Berkeley: University of California Press, 2007.

Daly, Herman. *Beyond Growth: The Economics of Sustainable Development*. Boston: Beacon Press, 1996.

Dean, Cornelia. "Survey Shows Gap Between Scientists and the Public," *The New York Times*, July 10, 2009.

Diamond, Jared. "What's Your Consumption Factor?" *The New York Times*, January 2, 2008.

Discussion Course on Choices for Sustainable Living. Portland, OR: Northwest Earth Institute, 2009.

"Ecological Disruption in Motion: A Briefing for Policymakers and Concerned Citizens on Audubon's Analyses of North American Bird Movements in the Face of Global Warming," *Audubon*, February 2009.

Fountain, Henry. "Researchers Find Bacteria That Devour Antibiotics," *The New York Times*, April 8, 2008.

Friedman, Thomas L. *Hot, Flat, and Crowded: Why We Need a Green Revolution and How It Can Renew America*. New York: Farrar Straus and Giroux, 2008.

Galbraith, Kate. "McKinsey Report Cites $1.2 Trillion in Potential Savings from Energy Efficiency," *The New York Times*, July 29, 2009.

Hartmann, Thom. *The Last Hours of Ancient Sunlight: Waking Up to Personal and Global Transformation*. New York: Harmony Books, 1998.

Hawken, Paul. *Blessed Unrest: How the Largest Movement in the World Came into Being and Why No One Saw It Coming*. New York: Viking Penguin, 2007.

Irvine, William B. *A Guide to the Good Life: The Ancient Art of Stoic Joy*. Oxford: Oxford University Press, 2009.

Kenneally, Christine. "The Inferno: Australia's Deadliest Fires Ever," *The New Yorker*, October 26, 2009.

Kolbert, Elizabeth. "The Climate of Man, " Parts 1-3, *The New Yorker*, April 25, May 2, and May 9, 2005.

_____. "The Darkening Sea: What Carbon Emissions Are Doing to the Ocean," *The New Yorker*, November 20, 2006.

_____. "Unconventional Crude: Canada's Synthetic-fuels Boom," *The New Yorker*, November 12, 2007.

_____. "The Catastrophist: NASA's Climate Expert Delivers the News No One Wants to Hear," *The New Yorker*, June 29, 2009.

_____. "Hosed: Is There a Quick Fix for the Climate?" *The New Yorker*, November 16, 2009.

Leakey, Richard and Roger Lewin. *The Sixth Extinction: Patterns of Life and the Future of Humankind*. New York: Anchor Books, 1996.

McKibben, Bill. *The End of Nature*. New York: Random House, 1989.

_____. *Deep Economy: The Wealth of Communities and the Durable Future.* New York: Times Books, 2007.

_____. "Beyond Radical: What Conservatives Could Bring to the Climate Conversation," *Orion*, July/August 2009.

_____. *Eaarth: Making a Life on a Tough New Planet.* New York: Times Books, 2010.

Montaigne, Fen. "The Ice Retreat: Global Warming and the Adélie Penguin," *The New Yorker*, December 21 & 28, 2009.

National Geographic, Vol. 217, No. 4 (April 2010): The Water Issue.

"Nobel Prize-Winning Scientists and Economists Call on Senate to Address Climate Change Now. More Than 2,000 Say Delay Will Worsen Consequences and Drive Up Costs," Press Release by Union of Concerned Scientists, March 11, 2010 (see also: http://www.ucsusa.org/global_warming/).

O'Neil, Kathleen. "Wildlife Need Help Surviving Climate Change Impacts," Press Release, National Parks Conservation Association, August 6, 2009.

Ponting, Clive. *A Green History of the World: The Environment and the Collapse of Great Civilizations.* New York: Penguin Group, 1993.

Pooley, Eric. *The Climate War: True Believers, Power Brokers, and the Fight to Save the Earth.* New York: Hyperion, 2010.

"Psychology and Global Climate Change: Addressing a Multi-faceted Phenomenon and Set of Challenges," A Report by the American Psychological Association's Task Force on the Interface Between Psychology and Global Climate Change, posted March 2010 (http://www.apa.org/science/climate-change).

Revkin, Andrew C. "Industry Ignored Its Scientists on Climate," *The New York Times*, April 24, 2009.

Rosenthal, Elisabeth. "Biofuels Deemed a Greenhouse Threat," *The New York Times*, February 8, 2008.

Speth, James Gustave. *Red Sky at Morning: America and the Crisis of the Global Environment.* New Haven: Yale University Press, 2004.

_____. *The Bridge at the Edge of the World: Capitalism, the Environment, and Crossing from Crisis to Sustainability.* New Haven: Yale University Press, 2008.

Tudge, Colin. *The Time Before History: Five Million Years of Human Impact.* New York: Scribner's, 1996.

Wilson, Edward O. *Biophilia*. Cambridge: Harvard University Press, 1984.

_____. *The Diversity of Life*. Cambridge: Harvard University Press, 1992.

_____. *The Future of Life*. New York: Alfred A. Knopf, 2002.

Worster, Donald. *Under Western Skies: Nature and History in the American West.* New York: Oxford University Press, 1992.

Yeatts, Loraine. "Plants Reported for the Table Mesas." Privately printed, 2001.